AUTHOR'S NOTE

This book was written as an educational learning piece for today's youth, not to glorify the street life in any way. Enjoy your read as it is filled with entertainment.

CAUGHT IN THE LIFE!

LONGEVITY PUBLISHING

Presents

CAUGHT IN THE LIFE!

BY

TEZ

VOLUME 1

Longevity Publishing, LLC
P.O. Box 346
Upper Darby, PA 19082
e-mail: longevityentertain@gmail.com

Amazon.com/Create Space

Follow Facebook@tezthewriter
Twitter@ tezthewriter
Instagram@ tezthewriter

Library of Congress Control Number:

ISBN: 978-0-692-02085-2

Cover Design/Graphics: Rachael Stockwell,
Clash Graphics info@clashgraphics.com

Author: TEZ

Editor-in-Chief: TEZ

Typesetter: Jane Eichwald, Ambler Document Processing,
jane@protypeexpress.com

Consulting: The Create Space Team

Published by Longevity Publishing

Printed in the United States of America

ACKNOWLEDGMENTS

First and foremost, all praise is due to Allah. Because without him none of this would have been possible. Secondly, my mother and dad, who have been in my corner since day one. I luv y'all. Grandmom & Grandpop I luv y'all for everything y'all ever done for me. Grandmom Gussie, my brothers: Gord and G3. My sisters: Nikki and Gina. My nieces: Roneeka, Alayshah, India and Nileah. My Aunts: Renee, Tee, Lydia, Ros, Bam, Gurly Carrie-Ann, and Shareefah. Cousins: Shea, Precious, Cookie (lil sis), Tirzah, Miyah, Pebbles, Tisha, Rasheeda, Tanya, Takia, Donnie, Khalil, Russell, Squirt, Rick, Marcus, Vinnie, Mont, Sule (A-G.A.M.E.). J.P. (Pickeep) you a monster on them beats. Your turn is coming. A.J. you already know the takeover is in progress. (A-G.A.M.E/Fanatick Family) Duke, you my heart youngin'. You got plenty potential. The Sky ain't even the limit for you. Stay focused on the court. Uncle Nelly & Big Russ (The Champ) 60th & Market Legends.

I begin this journey of writing the Caught in the Life series in 2004, which was 10 years ago. That was the year my big brother Markese inspired me to write this masterpiece. You're a genius bol. I luv you for that. Throughout the years of constant rejection letters by major and indie publishers, I never altered my vision and unwavering determination to win. I knew if I stayed patient and persistent that my dream would come true some day. It's not a word in the dictionary to describe how I feel at this moment. But, finally seeing my material in print, solidifies that you can do anything you want, if you put your mind to it. Shout out to President Obama. You proved that to be fact. You accomplished what most didn't believe could ever be a part of history.

I appreciate the publishers that paved the way for urban writers and gave me an opportunity to showcase my material: Donald Goines, Markese & Edna Jones, Dan Poynter, Malika Adero, Azarel, Teri Woods, Vickie Stringer, Nikki Turner, Mikell Davis, Sister Souljah, Shannon Holmes, Whahida Clark, Omar Tyree, Tiffany Womble, Literary Agent Marie Brown, Script consultant Leslie Paonessa and Joan Bressler, Senior Director of the Greater Philadelphia Film Office. My thanx is unconditional.

Shout out to the indie bookstores and distributors who keep our voices heard: Horizon Books (Ms. Xanell), Black And Noble (Hakim), Mejah Books (Ms. Elmlyn), Blackstar Music & Video (Harlem) and all the book clubs and bloggers on social media who show me love.

You're only as strong as your team. I want to thank my street and social media team over @ Longevity.

My graphic designer: Rachel Stockwell over @ Clash Graphics. You did ya thang. My editor and typesetter: Jane Eichwald.

My man Bunkin of Airtight Enterprises and manager of Philly's own recording artist: King Jaffi (The Future). History is in the making and it's going to be monumental. Shout out to my partner of Concept Kings Films: Larry Nicholson, producer of VH1's Love & Hip Hop New York, season 1 & 2. Manager of Nancy "Mama" Jones, Co-CEO of Powermove Multimedia, along with actor Flex Alexander and Karif Knox, creators of Americas Next Big Hit TV Show hosted by TJ Lavin and Chatt'n With Mama (reality show). Mama Jones can't wait to begin our project. Two dominant women a part of the Concept Kings movement: celebrity stylist, Kathy Rosa aka K.C. and Keba Jackson. L and Reef the TV and Movie lane is ours. Troy Carter, you went from a Def Jam exec to Eve's and Lady Gaga manager, then to the moon. I never forgot what you did for me. That was priceless. Congrats on your success. Party promoter: Cambodian Ali and his wife Kinisha of GS Entertainment and manager of rap artist, Cambodian Mitch along with Cambodian Chino, and my youngin' "A." My brother from another, Boo! Go out and get his book. It's fire! One Life! By Thomas "BOO!" Broaster. Cassius (25th St.) Hick. Also go and get my man Reem book. It's that work. Hidden Agendas by Kareem Torain. Shout out for just overturning your case. The Cooper & Domek family.

Mizzy (Mike), you know I couldn't forget you and Gene. Stevie Gee, Unk Ant and B_Rilla. It's levels to this s**t and y'all showin' em. E-marvelz, I luv you bol. You already know I got you. Only the strong survive. "F" is gone, but not forgotten. He was the #1 stunta!

Salute! Rue, the one and only (Real dude, last of a dying breed). Yock (54 The Ville) Inshallah you'll be home soon big bro. Sha (7th St.) Gino (G.Rap), Fly Ty, Lil Boo (Hemberger St.), Space Man, Lump, Fatta Banks, you already. Ronnie James, Bazz, Yak, Curly Tops: Braheem, Keem and "M" (Victory is near). Lucky Luchiano, Lue and his wife Nadia, Chop Chill, Al-Chill, Fest, Sheed, Nitty, Dog, Bill, Stink, Yank, Lil Stan, Kas, Lynwood, 01' head Monk, Sandman, Snakes, Ro, Tek, Staaf, Stanka Man, Turtle, D.P., Hov, A.B., Dre, T.R., E' (38th St.) Cliff, Sniffles (Summer St PJ's.) My man Saudi repping North Carolina, Rude Boy (Glen) Good dude. Jay Raw (Uptown) 01 head Gorgie Boy, Thatch, I appreciate the support homie. Lil Tuffy, Littles, Fat Cat, Hak, Mont (muscles) Candy Man, Snoop, Wiz, G-buckz, Reds, Stink (Abdul Hak) & Rafir keep your faith in Allah and stay strong. Click (11th & Cumberland) My youngin' Jay (Uptown) Adolph, Face, Nard, Saeed, Daryl Schuler, Visa (Uptown), Popa, Lemon, Cook, Teeb, Trinny AKA Show (BX), 6-9, Coonie Fox, Fatty, Woo, Bop, Shakim (EdenWald), Dutch (BK) & KB (Queens) my NY Boyz.

Qadree, Lihtz Kamraz and the whole Fanatick Family. Lihtz you a problem and you next to blow. Put the city on ya back, youngin'. BigRubeHarley@streetgazing.com, "Sixx-King," Spade O, Sparks, Goldie, Nina Ross, Dutch, Cool-C, Schooly-D, Seigel, Freeway, Jack Frost, Charlie Mack, Tiff (Charli Baltimore), We Run the Streets, HeadShots, DJ Diamond Kuts, Ms. Cat, 01' head Biz: Bat Cave Radio, Kev Sanchez (Tanna The Beast) Beards in the Building

Movement. You know we go way back to the Brook days. Rapping in chiphers and banging on tables. You already know where the luv is at. Black (Frankford), Bernard Hopkins (B-Hop) you held it down for the city on the boxing side. Plus you came from behind these same walls. Salute! Living legend. It's only right to pay homage to the industry lifeline of the city. Tereza, V a very talented writer. Look out for her book: Jazz 1 Cafe. Lil Crystal thanx for the critique. Naeema, you always been thoro, Boonie, Muffy, Dee, Keisha, Kamil, Shahaddah, Nafeesa, Renee keep writing. Darcele (Nikki), Tinika, Lucy, Tysha (Baby Doll), Toya, Shonda, Tyesha (Dimples), Lakenna (Dimples), Tori, Dardy, Yeep, Gambling Lisa, Smyles, Erica, Brandy, Summer, Sundy, Mireille, Sareeta, Marlise, Passion, Sparkle, Tammy, Keisha, Joy, Aminah and Aaliyah Small.

Shout out to the playas who lost their lives to the struggle: Mikey-"F", Vell (Mackavelli), Kevin Jones, Little-Man, Genie Boy, Macky Woods, Boo Burger, Dump Truck, Reemie Scarfo, Hasheen, Littles, Pumpkin, Lil Walt, Furr, Andy, Crack, Jizz, B-Bubble, Basil, Devon, Boo-Cherry, Bub, Taalib, Booza, Pie Face Tone, Lil Gary, Mikey-"A", Mike Skully, Lil Rob, Raeneil, D'ivee, Naeem, Lil Joey, Sabir, Mikal (Uncle Mickey), Uncle Half, Suga Bear, Doc Jordan, Reese, Mont, Shaheed, Uncle Ed, Q.B., Dontae, Shannon, Black Dame, Tat, Muff, Quran, Manny, Don Wuan, Butta, Buzz, Tone Jackson, Titty, Stoney, June Fox and Pop. You are all gone but not forgotten, believe that.

Last but not least I appreciate all my loyal readers and online followers who support me. I do this for y'all. I promise to keep pumping out heat. I know so many people. So if I forgot your name, just remind me and I'll put you in my Vol. 2 shout outs.

This series is dedicated to those riding with me from day one and those who counted me out—count me in. The pinnacle of success is the epitome of hard work and dedication—you can't stop a machine.

.

PART 1

COMING OF AGE

CHAPTER 1

It was a scorching hot summer of 91' in the city of Philadelphia in a section known as "West Philly," where fiends or smokers dwelled as most called the crack addicts, despite the sight of innocence of boys playing in the water from fire hydrants to girls jumping rope. In the mist of it all, the customers would form ten people units, awaiting to be served crack by the youngsters who manned their post. These were once regular people with talent, who hit rock bottom from their addiction. Crack cocaine was a new epidemic that took America by storm, mainly attacking the intercity ghettos. Individuals on crack would literally sell anything that wasn't nailed down. Nintendo's would disappear out of homes. Leather jackets grew legs of their own, walking out of clothing stores as rental cars sometimes never found their way back to the rental agencies. This epidemic turned some of the baddest women out. Some which even went from wearing top of the line mink coats, to driving around in their cars, trying to give the corner hustlers sex for a couple chunks of crack. This untamable monster provided the street hustlers a new rapid way of getting rich and Jamal also known as Malley, watched it all unfold as a youngin'. This was the year he was introduced to the game, a game that wasn't to be taken lightly. A game that didn't love nobody, but catered to all. Malley and his cousins, Lil J' and Kaeem always stuck together. When you saw one you saw them all. They actually moved like real brothers, so if they trusted anybody it was each other.

Their older cousin Rod, who stood five feet nine inches, slim built, light brown with a bald head, controlled 62nd & Market. Market Street was where most of his drugs were sold. Rod and Malley's Aunt Rita who was Kaeem and Lil J's mom lived right around the corner. Rod taught them small things about the game, but never wanted them in it. Each of them were slick, but not slick enough for the fast life, which was dealing with things on a whole different level. The game had it's advantages and disadvantages and understanding the pros and cons were ninety-five percent of it. Besides getting money you had to watch out for the cops and those who worked for the cops. Then you had stick up boys who would try some people, then some who would try anybody. These were the ones you had to make an example out of immediately, to send a message that you weren't going to be pegged as soft. If not, these guys would be at your doorsteps day and night looking forward to reap your earnings. This was how Rod and his team maneuvered, having six corners already sold up. On each corner he had thirty one illusions and dime bags of powder in the bars. He was moving two bricks a week, bringing in anywhere from $50,000 to $65,000. He literally had

Market Street in the palm of his hands. He used a little cut if any at all. This made his product top of the line. If it wasn't Rod's product, the fiends didn't want it. He treated them good and didn't disrespect them because they were getting high. Rod had a few hot cars: a 1990 Saab, a red Cherokee with a black rag top, which was equipped with colorful lights underneath the bottom that lit up at night. His prize possession was his cocaine white 190-E Mercedes Benz with hammers. Basically he was the man, he picked up being flamboyant from how J.B.M. used to roll through the city. The neighborhood loved him as he made sure the elderly had food and paid the young bucks to keep their pavements swept. He wanted to see to it that the neighbors had a little love for him, even though he was doing wrong. Rod kept his women in Dolphin earrings, Louis Vuitton and Gucci from head to toe. As M.C.M. was fading out he styled from time to time in Alpina's, Porsha Design and Sergio tech sweat suits. He owned three hair salons: one on 52nd & Market, 52nd & Parkside and 60th & Lansdowne. These were three major strips where most players hung out around. Rod was a genius for opening the salons in those areas. The money he was getting was every hustler in the neighborhood dream.

Malley and his mom lived on 55th & Vine in a two-story project known as Summer Street. This part of "West Philly" was rough. Just like any other project, there were roaches, graffiti and the smell of urine filtering the air. The hustlers from Summer Street would also have fiends lined up on the "Wall" serving them. It was no escaping how hard crack hit the streets.

3

Everywhere Malley looked somebody was getting money. His mother was doing all she could do as a single parent and being on welfare. His father had also got sucked into the wave of smoking crack and before long he would be nowhere to be found. As a written rule it's nearly impossible to raise a man. Taking care of the bills and trying to raise him was difficult. The thought of knowing what his mom was doing to maintain for them, haunted his mind every night. He was the only child with no real source of income other then preparing to work for Phil-A-Job in the summer.

This was his last year of Shoemaker. This middle school was a small fashion show. His first two years was rough for him, having to keep switching his shirts and pants to try and throw the females off and even that got played out. He was tired of wearing the same Timberlands and Standsmith Adidas. Malley was getting away with his looks. The handsome young man stood five foot seven inches, light brown and 147 pounds, but the females at Shoemaker wouldn't stay interested in guys if they couldn't keep up with their appearance.

This pressure had him trying to keep up with the Joneses. With less than six months to graduate and his mother still struggling, he was afraid that he wasn't going to be able to be in the graduation and yearbook. This alone had him stressing. His mentality was to figure out an angle and figure out one fast.

Kaeem and Lil J's parents worked, so they practically wanted for nothing. Although they were his aunt and uncle, they had their own bills to pay. Every week Malley would stay over his Aunt Rita's house where it was going down. It was nothing but, money up and down 62nd Street. Rod had maintained his corners and fame in the city. Malley started to want to become like his older cousin. He was getting tired of having next to nothing in his pocket. The spud games was just keeping him with lunch money. The sight of seeing the young bucks from Southwest and those who hustled for Rod, driving squatters to school made his appetite for the game grow. Catching the bus to school anymore was out of the question. The game begin to cave in on him.

CHAPTER 2

It was that Sunday night around 9:00 p.m. when Malley decided to call Kaeem and Lil J'. He needed some money and Rod was the only way. The phone rang a few times before it was answered.

"Hello?" Kaeem answered.

"What's up?" Malley stated.

"Who this?" Kaeem asked again, uncertain of the voice.

"Man, this Mal," he reaffirmed.

"Oh, what's up cousin?" He re-expressed his excitement.

"The game Ka', it's time to turn it up," Malley stated in a serious tone.

"The game? What you went crazy?" Kaeem replied.

"Ka' I'm twisted, y'all cool."

"You know what Rod said come with the game. That's out of our league. It's consequences in that," Kaeem stated.

"Man, life is about takin' risks. If we don't reach for what we want, what we want won't be put in our reach. Ya feel me?" Malley said, trying to get his point across.

"Malley, you trippin."

"No, I'm starvin'. I'm tired of havin' the hunger to get money. I ain't talkin' no more, I'm movin'."

"Yeeeah," Kaeem stated.

"Yeah, mom duke is back in her bills. She don't got it for me to graduate. I gotta come through crushin'. My dinner dance comin' up. I'm tryna bus Simone from Parkside and Turquoise from Wynnfield. You know they the baddest chicks in Shoe," he said making his intentions clear.

Simone and Turquoise was two beautiful females. Simone was about five feet four inches, red bone with a crazy body. Her hair was jet black and long. She had pink lips to match her complexion. The way her eyebrows grew, blended right in with her narrow face. Turquoise on the other hand had a caramel complexion with good hair to the root with turquoise eyes to complement her name. She was five feet five inches with a body to kill for. Her skin was just so clear. Malley just had to have her.

"Damn, Malley you serious huh?"

"Yeah, dead serious."

"How you gonna get up the money?" Kaeem asked curiously, not knowing what kind of plan he had mapped out.

"I'ma get with Rod."

"Rod? Rod ain't gonna give you no work. You know he told us to stay away from the game."

"Man, I got this. I can't ask my mom to get his number, so I need you to get it for me."

"How I'ma get it?"

"Easy, you gonna see him before me. I know I don't hear Lil J' laughing?"

"Yup, he think you went crazy."

"Tell him I said when I come off, don't be tellin' them chicks he know me."

"Mal, I got the number, but don't tell him I gave it to you."

"Alright, alright, I got you," he said, eager to get the number.

"You got a pen and piece of paper?" Kaeem asked.

"Yeah, go 'head," he replied.

"878-3180. You ain't get it from me."

"How many times you gonna say that? I got you."

"Alright, later."

"Alright." They both hung up the phone.

Kaeem was worried about how Rod was going to feel about him giving Malley his number regardless of them all being family. Rod had never got into depth about him and Malley doing business, so it was a shot in the dark. Malley needed to gather his thoughts to see how he was going to approach his older cousin for drugs to pay for his graduation, dinner dance and yearbook photos. Of course, he would need pocket money as well. He hesitated for a few hours until he mustered up enough nerve to call him. He finally picked up the phone and reached out. The phone rang as he anticipated his answer. The first two rings went unanswered which seemed like forever. The phone rang two more times before that familiar voice he longed to hear answered.

"Hello?" Rod asked as he answered.

"Yo," Malley stated.

"Who's this?" he questioned.

"This Mal," he replied.

"Who?" he questioned again.

"Malley."

"Who?"

"Jamal, your lil cousin, man," he said, kind of frustrated.

"Oh, damn what's up lil cousin? Is everythin' alright?" Rod asked out of concern.

"I gotta speak with you."

"I'll be through Aunt Rita's later. And how you get this number?" he asked, just when Malley thought he was out in the clear.

"Ka' gave it to me." He threw Kaeem right under the bus, hoping Rod wasn't upset about contacting him out of the blue. Rod knew something was up, being as though he couldn't wait to see him amongst the family.

"That's right, I got somethin' to do later, so I'ma have to get with you tomorrow. I don't talk on these horns like that," Rod stated. Malley needed to think on his toes.

"Ay Rod, can you come scoop me from school tomorrow?" he asked, hoping he would say yes.

"Where you at?"

"Shoe," he replied.

"What time you get out?"

"Like 2:45, three."

"Alright, I'll be there," he said as he was curious about what was so important that he needed to speak with him so urgently. Showing interest in coming to meet, Malley gave him a sign of hope.

CHAPTER 3

"*A*lright," Malley replied. He couldn't wait until tomorrow. Rod really had no idea how much Malley admired him. Malley sort of came from a long line of hustlers. His Uncle Rosco who got murdered in the mid-80's, had the Mantua section of "West Philly," sold up. He was over the top with everything he did. More people feared him, than loved him. His problem was he never mastered how to balance the two. He allowed the fear to outweigh the love, which was most likely the key to his demise. Well, that's how the streets told it anyway. Malley and his Uncle Rosco's relationship wasn't the greatest, because him and his mother practically hated each others guts. This tension put a major strain on their uncle to nephew bond. Honestly, this was a small part of why Malley wanted to be a hustler and reality was that nobody was helping him and his mother. She was only able to do so much and affording the clothes he really wanted to wear was out of the question. Surely, any mother wants the best for their child, but she was confined by their circumstances. From time to time, Malley would cast blame on his uncle for failing to put aside some money for him and his mom, being as though he knew his dad wasn't in his life. He figured had he left them a cushion to sit on, they probably wouldn't be going through these financial problems.

Up until this day nobody knew where the rest of the money was. The kidnappers only got $150,000. The streets has it that Rosco was an undercover millionaire. His murder was the most horrendous homicide the streets of "Philly" saw since 85' when Moneybags and his right hand man Littles were found riddled with bullets in a "North Philly" abandoned basement. Whomever the kidnappers were who snatched Rosco were all business. They severed his fingers, cut his throat from ear to ear, then shot him in the head multiple times. This was surely a death penalty case, but a case that would never see the light of day in a courthouse. No one talked, so no one was ever charged or convicted. Malley was too young to understand why his uncle was murdered so gruesomely. The fact of the matter was that the drug game breeds these types of animals, who would take your head off with no problem about money. The way his uncle was taken out found its way back to his mind as he pondered entering the game. But, in his mind how could that type of calamity come his way when he's just in it to earn a few dollars to pay for his graduation and stay afloat while he attends school. Although he tried, it was no way he could really compare his house income to Kaeem and Lil J's, because at the end of the day they were a little more fortunate than him. After brainstorming for hours on end and anticipating meeting with Rod, he couldn't fight back the urge to tell Kaeem what had transpired, so he called him despite the time of night.

"Hello?" Kaeem answered, after struggling with picking the phone up.

"Yo, what it is Ka'?" he asked.

"What it is? Mal, it's 3:00 a.m. in the morning," Kaeem replied, agitated that Malley woke him up out of his sleep.

"Look, I wanted to let you know I got with Rod today."

"I know you ain't call me this time of night to tell me that. If my mom would of picked this phone up she would have been snappin."

"I know, my bad. It's on Ka', it's on," he said.

"Alright, tell me all about it tomorrow," Kaeem said mumbling. He hung up, then shook his head, leaving Malley with a dial tone to listen to.

* * * * *

All day in school Malley was just staying to himself. He just secretly longed for everyone to see him with his big cousin. Everybody and their mother either knew who Rod was, or had somehow heard of him. Being seen with him would definitely boost his status in the eyes of those he went to school with. At his age it was harmless to front here and there. Two forty-five p.m. came and school let out. It was crowded as usual, especially it being a nice day. Majority of everybody stood across the street in front of the Conestoga Street Recreation Center. This is where neighborhood basketball games took place. The remaining individuals either stood on the side of Shoemaker or across from the main entrance. Malley watched as some departed on foot or by vehicle, but all he was worried about was where Rod was at. From a distance "Road to the Riches," by Kool G. Rap & Polo, a song all too familiar, traveled through the air, snatching his attention along with everyone else's as they could hear the music get closer and closer. Whomever it was had a knocking car system. As the music became clear, so did the cocaine white 190-E Mercedes Benz Rod turned the corner in. Malley could almost do a back flip. Rod had kept his promise and all eyes were on him and Malley as he pulled up to him like the boss he was. This was his moment and everybody he wanted to see him, saw him. Malley opened the door and got in. As he scoured the crowd nonchalantly, he noticed that Simone and Turquoise's eyes were glued on him while they pulled off. A sense of relief came over him as the perception he wanted painted was captured.

CHAPTER 4

"What's up youngin'?"

"Look Rod. I know you don't want us in the game, but my situation is different."

"Different then what?" he questioned.

"Different than, Ka' and Lil J's. My mom is back in her bills and you know my pop left us twisted. I can't really get a real gig."

"You know auntie know what time it is. All she gotta do is say the word and I'll make sure she get that doe. But then again you know she ain't takin' this type of money," said Rod pleading his case.

"I know, you know she works with a lot of pride. My graduation and dinner dance is comin' up and I doubt if she'll be able to pay for either of them."

"I feel you. Here take this five hundred and put it to the side. This should cover what you need to take care of," Rod said after he reached in his pocket and pulled out a stack of money. Malley was content that he gave him the money for his graduation and dinner dance but deep down he craved for something much more. Rod took him to get something to eat with him from Long Acres eatery on 60th Street. After they ate their famous barbecue chicken he dropped Malley off so he could take care of his usual business.

Malley had another agenda on his to do list. He knew that once he paid for his graduation and dinner dance he would basically be back to square one, barely surviving with just enough lunch money in his pocket. He definitely didn't want to go back to the basics, so he came up with an idea to double the money Rod gave him. He had heard about how he could double his money by getting a double up in crack from the bol Tuck who was doing his thing on 57th & Ludlow. Time was of the essence and that was something he wasn't going to waste. He took his mountain bike, took the $500 Rod gave him and rode down to 57th & Ludlow to buy a $1,000 worth of crack. They gave it to him capped up already in 31 illusions capsules. He took the bundle of crack, stuffed it in his backpack and rode his bike back home.

He rode like a mad man. He was literally scared too death, but the rush gave him a feeling he never felt before. When he got home he bucked straight to his room to see what he had scored. He locked his door in case his mother decided to appear unannounced, then unwrapped the plastic it came in. As he got the plastic off of the package, he examined the capsules, the beige looking crack was bottled up in. The problem was that he didn't have no way of selling it because he had no clientele. Malley had never sold a piece of drug a day in his life, so he didn't know how much each cap was sold for. He just knew that the amount of crack he had was supposed to bring him back a $1,000 in money. As he was soring through his work a sound of his doorknob being turned snatched him out of his zone, followed by a few knocks on the door. It was a good thing he locked it before he scoured through his package.

"Jamal?" questioned his mother.

"Huh?" he replied panicking, trying to scramble to put away his drugs.

"Boy open this door," she demanded, as he could still hear the doorknob trying to be turned.

"Here I come," he said making sure everything was put away.

"Boy what was you doing?" she asked.

"I dozed off for a minute," he said quickly, concocting a lie.

"Umm-hmm. I want to talk to you about something."

"About what?" he said, getting on the defensive. He felt as though she could see right through him, knowing that he was up to something.

"About them fresh tail little girls calling my house all times of the night. I'm not going to have that. On school nights no calls after eleven and on weekends, twelve," she said sternly.

"Come on mom. I'm gettin' older," he replied, basically feeling a sign of relief that it wasn't what he thought it was.

"Getting older my butt. You heard what I said. I don't care how their parents raise them, but I know how I'm going to raise mines," she spoke.

"Alright mom," Malley said, not wanting to hear his mother preach to him about girls. He wanted to get back to figuring how he was going to get rid of his drugs.

"Don't alright me. I mean it Jamal," she stated again.

"Okay."

"Alright, you know mommy loves you," his mother said, pinching his cheek before leaving. He hated that his mother still treated him as a mommy's boy.

CHAPTER 5

The next day he went down his Aunt Rita's house right after school. He took about twenty caps with him to see how much they were worth on the streets and how could he move them. The first people he showed was none other than Kaeem and Lil J'. They went downstairs in the basement so they could hear when their parents came home. They weren't about to let them catch them with drugs in the house. As they locked the door Malley opened his Ziploc bag that contained a few capsules and placed them on the table.

"Damn where you get that at?" Lil J' asked.

"I made a move."

"You wasn't playin' huh?"

"Naw."

"Rod passed off?" Kaeem asked.

"Naw, he gave me a couple dollars. I just took what he gave me and grabbed some work."

"He know about that?" Lil J' asked.

"Hell no. He'd probably feel some type of way," said Malley.

"You know he will, especially if he find out," spoke Kaeem.

"Yeah, I know," Malley said.

"So how are you gonna get rid of it?" asked Lil J'.

"How else. Take it to the streets," Malley said with confidence.

"Take it to what streets?" Kaeem questioned.

"Market Street," said Malley.

"You think you gonna be able to pump ya package on 62nd Street without Rod findin' out?" asked Kaeem.

"Why not?" Malley answered naively.

"Cuz, you playin' with fire," spoke Lil J'.

"Like Rod is gonna do somethin' to his little cousin," said Malley.

"You're crazy," said Kaeem.

"No, I'm hungry."

"You know how much each cap go for?" Kaeem questioned.

"Nope, but we about to find out," replied Malley.

"We? What do you mean we?" said Lil J'.

"All I need y'all to do is watch my back while I ask a fiend what each cap go for," Malley insisted.

"Alright, we got you cuz," Kaeem reassured.

Malley put the caps back in the bag to begin his expedition. Him, Kaeem and Lil J' took to Market Street combing the neighborhood customers. They first had to find a fiend who didn't have no money. As they walked from 62nd & Market, they cut up Dewey Street to 62nd & Arch where they were able to run into two fiends coming from Larry Gunther's house. Larry Gunther was an original leader of the infamous Moon Gang from back in the seventies, who had got hooked on crack. His house was the smoke house for all the fiends. Skip and Sandy, two neighborhood fiends, were in route to find money to get another hit. As they headed towards Malley's direction, he mustered up enough nerve to approach them with a head nod to see if they wanted something.

"What's up?" Malley asked.

"We ain't got no money right now. But what you got?" asked Skip. He was the neighborhood thief. He could steal a doughnut from out of a cop car. That's how good he was. If you needed something Skip was the man.

"I got that good shit," Malley said, opening his palm that he held a few caps clinched in. Skip and Sandy's eyes got huge as they gawked at the yellow top 31 illusions. Their mouths watered at the sight of the beige coke, only hoping to achieve their fix to stop the craving.

"Oh, I see, you do got the good shit," Sandy said, moving back and forth, rubbing her palms together. She wasted no time trying to run her little game. She begin to skits, starting to scratch her scalp through her tightly wrapped scarf. Lil J' and Kaeem made sure they kept an eye out for the police, as this was a highly drug trafficking area.

"What you got trays or duces?" Skip asked wanted to know if the caps were sold for two dollars or three dollars. This is what Malley needed to know. What was the drugs he had worth on the streets.

"Trays," he guessed, hoping it was the right answer.

"Won't you let us get right so we can know what you got, because Rod got the best shit around here,"

Sandy said. Malley, Lil J' and Kaeem all looked at each other at the same time. With cars constantly driving by and neighbors attending to their affairs, Malley wanted to elude the sight of "Town Watch." Although a lot of crack was being sold, it didn't negate the fact that it was always some nosy neighbors peeking out their blinds, ready to call the police at the sight of a sell. So a little nervousness from Malley could only be expected.

"Come on get us started. We know people, if it's good we can get rid of it," spoke Skip, trying to convince him that they were the ones who could help him move his package. Malley continued to ponder as he looked Skip up and down in his dirty clothes that appeared to have been worn for a week straight. Rather it being his clothes or the way they smelled. It convinced him to take their invitation. The only people that know the streets is the ones who roamed the streets.

"Alright, hold up," Malley said, looking at Kaeem uncertain.

"Let us see what you're working with," said Skip, growing impatient.

"Yeah, let us see," Sandy said, anxiously hoping they could get a freebie.

"Here, take these," Malley said, giving them a cap a piece.

"We gonna do these and let you know what you got," spoke Skip, ready to get down to business. They each took a cap and went into the alley. Kaeem, Lil J' and Malley watched them from afar. They would just move around a little, so it wouldn't seem like they were selling drugs. Only after a minute elapsed, they could see Sandy and Skip shooting out of the alley like bats out of hell, flagging them down. Malley didn't really know what to think. He just hoped it was good news.

"What's up?" Malley asked.

"Goddamn that was some good shit," said Skip, grinding his teeth together.

"Yeah, you got more?" questioned Sandy with her eyes large as fifty cent pieces.

"Yeah, but it's for sell. I got y'all started, now get me started," Said Malley now knowing that he had some good product.

"Alright, we're on our job. Come on Sandy," Skip said eager to take off.

"What's your name baby?" she asked.

"M." Malley replied.

"Alright, M, we gonna run 'em in," Sandy reassured. Her and Skip took off towards Cobbs Creek. They were probably going to steal from up 69th Street and try to run into their buddies who also smoked coke.

That day Skip and Sandy kept their word. They helped Malley get rid of the little bit of package that he had with him in no time. And in return he rewarded them with a few caps a piece. The unfortunate part was that the money continued to come and Malley was out.

CHAPTER 6

All he could think about was the next day as he saw how fast he could make some money. As two days went by, he was ready to re-up again, this time getting three double up's. Malley started to feel good having his own money in his pocket. He was flipping his own packs. He was his own boss and nobody expected him to be hustling so he was far from hot. Being as though he didn't want to really involve Kaeem and Lil J', he didn't ask them to lookout for him anymore while he served the customers. He took it upon himself to look out.

Rod had gotten word that it was someone moving drugs on his corners and of course it didn't sit well with him, but for some reason he could never catch the culprit his fiends would tell him about. All he knew was that their name was "M." Nobody was going to sell on Rod's corner other than the workers he put there. Sixty-second Street was his and his alone. Although this didn't hurt his pockets, he viewed it as a respect thing. Unknowing to Malley that Rod was on to someone out there selling on his corners, who was him. He stayed motivated with moving his double up's.

Rainy days couldn't even slow him down. He stood out in the rain with his Columbian rain suit and black chukka Timberlands on making sure the fiends got their fix. This was when the most money came as Malley could catch most of the traffic on their way to Larry Gunther house. Bobby Cool who was also a neighborhood fiend used his house as a place for the smokers to get high. Rod would put drugs in his house from time to time when Larry's crib was hot. Malley stayed posted on Robinson Street between Arch & 62nd. This way he could see everything moving from the intersection, even the police.

"Right here, right here," Malley said as he called a few fiends headed towards the crack house direction.

"We're okay baby," spoke the lady accompanied with a friend trying to get to their destination.

"Look, I got them plays for days," he said, approaching her with his hand, showing her his product.

"What you got?" she asked, now seeming concerned.

"Tray's. How many you want?" he asked.

"Can I get seven for twenty?" she questioned.

"All day. Matter fact, here go another one. Make sure you run 'em in. I'ma be right here," Malley said as he gave her some extras.

"Alright," she said taking off happy with her friend, who never said a word.

Malley pretty much got the swing of things from the time he put in on them corners. Giving out extras was the move of a smart hustler. This was how he got his clientele larger. He tried to stop as many people from going to the cribs as he could. Some remained loyal, some gave him a play. He managed to move most of his work. As he had gotten down to his last $100 pack, things began to slow up and the rain began to pick up. He knew it was time to pack it up, so he went to his stash spot in a tire that hid in the bushes to get his work. How bad was his timing because as soon as he went to remove his stash, a police car slowly crept by Robinson Street. As the car continued to roll, he almost was certain that the cop had seen him near the bushes what probably appeared to look suspicious. Thinking on his toes, he quickly walked towards Arch Street trying to see which way the car was headed. He could see the back of the car reversing. Malley immediately threw his pack under a car as he kept walking. The cop put his car in park and jumped out aggressively.

"What the fuck you doin' out here?" the cop asked.

"I'm goin' to the store," Malley replied.

"What was you doin' by them bushes?" the cop questioned.

"I was tyin' my shoes." He spoke quick on his toes.

"Yeah, okay. Get against the wall," he stated. Throwing Malley against the wall, he started to pat him down roughly. Malley was a bit nervous hoping this badge heavy cop didn't find his pack.

"Officer, my mom is gonna be waitin' on me," he said trying to play the young buck card. Malley had bigger things to worry about. He got rid of his package but not the money.

"That's Officer Mankings to you and what do we have here?" the cop asked, pulling out a wad of money from Malley's pocket.

"Money," spoke Malley.

"Yeah, I know it's money, but who's money?" he asked.

"My mom money," he answered.

"Five hundred in wet money? Man this a Puerto Rican knot. You out here sellin' huh? This my money. Now take a fuckin' walk. I catch you out here again tonight, you're goin' to jail." he told him as he grabbed him by his neck and threw him off the wall. All Malley could do but shake his head because it was nothing he could do. He had encountered the taste of a dirty cop. He could only hope that he didn't find his stash.

A double loss would definitely hurt. He kept taking sneak peeks back at the cop to see if he pulled off. He walked all the way to Market Street just to play it safe. Once he seen that the coast was clear, he took the long route to get back to his package that was a little wet, but untouched. Malley took a deep breath just being glad he didn't take that double loss.

Instead of taking heed and calling it a night, Malley's mind was elsewhere. He didn't want to go in without no money in his pockets, so he stayed on Market Street, this time trying to catch some sells. One of his usual customers came to him wanting some work. Malley directed him near the alley. As he went to serve him, he could hear car tires screeching, followed by doors being opened. By the time he tried to turn around, all he could see was the chrome from the gun that was pointed at him. The fiend that had set Malley up had eased off of the scene.

"Don't turn around. Who you out here sellin' for?" the hooded culprit asked.

"Nobody, me," Malley said, scared too death. He had to respect that these culprits had the drop on him. It was pretty much nothing he could do. He had never been in this position before. All he could do was pray that this wasn't the end of his life.

"I'ma ask you again, or I'ma pop you in your leg. Who you out here sellin' for?" he asked again, more sternly.

"Me, man. I got my own stuff," he stated with his hands up in the air trying to turn around to see who was behind him.

"You think I'm playin'?" he said sternly.

"No, it's mines. I'm gettin' double up's," said Malley, pointing to his pack.

"From who? You know this Rod shit out here?" he questioned.

"I know, that's my cousin," Malley replied, hoping that would get him out of this situation.

"Yeah, right. I'm pop you for playin' wit our strip," he said, cocking the gun back.

"Hold up, hold up. Take your hood off," Rod said as the voice began to sound all too familiar. As Malley took his hood off, Rod became furious as Malley's face was revealed.

"What's up, give me the word," his henchman stated, anxious to put some work in.

"Man it's my little dick head ass cousin. What the fuck you doin' out here, you coulda just got killed?" Rod questioned as his henchman slowly put his gun away.

"I was just tryin' to get a couple dollars," he replied.

"I gave you some doe. Man get the fuck in the car," he said, grabbing Malley by the back of his neck, throwing him in the back seat. Rod was mad that it was his little cousin that he was out there looking for. Malley knew he had really pissed him off. He knew his best bet was to keep quiet, at least for the time being.

"Youngin' you was almost a memory. This shit ain't to be played with out here," Rod's henchman spoke, pulling off watching his surroundings as they departed from the empty corners of Market Street driving into the night. Rod showed Malley how easy it was for him to touch anybody who tried to impinge on his territory.

CHAPTER 7

The next day Rod wasted no time sitting Malley down. He was still a bit irate that it was his little cousin who was cutting into his rations and wanted to get into the game. But his entire mentality was that if Malley was going to be in the game, he was going to play the game right. Rod had taken him to one of his low-key spots over Southwest. Every crib he had was laid out from the furniture to the TVs to the feet sinking Persian rugs. When you entered one of his pads you were going to feel the presence of taste. The presence of greatness. The presence of a boss. The finest of women couldn't even resist the temptation of keeping their clothes on. Malley secretly longed for his cousin's lifestyle and he wasn't alone because a few other players in the city did as well.

"I ain't mean to grip you up, but you pissed me off," Rod said, being apologetic.

"I can dig it. I should of told you what I was doin,' " said Malley, understanding why he felt the way he felt and did what he did.

"Man that's water under the bridge. You family at the end of the day. You know why I brought you here, right?" Rod questioned.

"Kind of. It gotta be about me grindin'?" Malley asked.

"You're on point. I thought about last night and I thought about when I first chased the game. Chasin' you away is only gonna make you chase it harder. We had our talk before so I already know where you're comin' from. My thing is this. You think you ready for this game and everythin' that comes wit it?" Rod asked, waiting to see if Malley could at least begin to comprehend the magnitude of this loveless monster.

"I don't know, but I know I'm ready to get this money," he replied.

"I know that you went and got your own package. I know you ain't have no problem settin' up shop on my shit," said Rod, with a slight snicker.

"It wasn't like that," he said.

"Like what? You think the next man gonna cut you a break, when he catch you out on his corner flippin' your shit?" he asked.

"Naw," Malley answered.

"So know it's rules in this shit. I'm not gonna stop you from hustlin'. If you ready to get money, we gonna get it together," spoke Rod.

"I feel you. I'm ready," answered Malley.

"Alright, this is how we're gonna do it. I'ma front you an ounce and whatever you buy I'ma match it. I'ma show you how to get this paper," Rod explained, rubbing his palms together.

"I'm wit it," Malley quickly responded.

"Only on one condition," he said.

"What's that?" he questioned.

"You gotta go to school. You don't go to school, you won't be hustlin' nowhere. Not for me, yourself, nobody. The posts is already doin' it. All you gotta do is maintain it. I'ma put some youngin's out there to look out for 5-0 and the jammie boys," spoke Rod, giving him a small layout of how he was going to run the operation.

"Alright, when I start?" Malley asked.

"Listen to you askin' when you start like this shit is legit. On weekdays your shifts gonna be four to nine, this way auntie won't be trippin' on you. On the weekends you can pull all-nighters. The more you can move, the more I'ma drop on you," Rod expressed. He wasn't going to force his hand to take on more than he could handle, but he let him know that it was available.

"That's what's up," he replied.

"You know the three parts of the game?" Rod asked.

"No, what's the parts?" he questioned.

"You can be rich, dead or in jail. The goal is to get rich. If you ain't focused and on top of your game, bad things can happen. If 5-0 ever grab you, no matter what, tell 'em nothin'. They only know what you tell 'em. In this game you keep your mouth shut. What happens in the streets stay in the streets, you understand?" he questioned firmly.

"Yeah," he responded.

"I keep lawyers on speed dial. They'll have you out before the cops who locked you up shift is over," he said, reassuring Malley causing him to crack a smile, now making him feel totally convinced that his big cousin had his best interest at heart. School was definitely in session and he was ready to learn. This was the first time the game was given to him so he was beyond all ears. He explained to Malley that the stick up boys was always out to tax and to beware because he may encounter some. Depending on the situation, Rod was seasoned enough to read rather he had to respect the drop and give them what they came for, or try their chin and reverse the drop. However, it played out retaliation was going to be a must. This is what he embedded in Malley's head. He sat there, not saying a word and trying to take in as much as possible. Rod next covered another part of the game. One of the most important parts; the chicks. He went into depth on how women are infatuated with the glamour and glitz that the players of the game possess. How Malley was about to have damn near every female in school paying attention to him outside of Simone and Turquoise. So having a main chick on his hip would be a good thing as long as they had respect for him and not the money he was getting. Once reaching a certain level, it's hard seeing past a chick's greed who's a product of the game. He forewarned him of the evils and traps. Rod was dealing Malley the cards and it was his job to play his hand right. He gave him a beeper and whip to get around in. It was on and Malley could feel it. He might have been the only young bol in West Philly pushing a Lincoln LSC to school. It wasn't brand new but he was about to make a major statement.

CHAPTER 8

The first two months went by smoothly. Malley used Ms. Margie's house to bag up in and cook. Rod made sure he had his young bol L.A. show him how to cook it, weight it and cap it. They were able to bring back extras using thirty one illusions. This enabled them to really see some money for themselves. Malley stacked most of what he earned. He didn't have to spend a lot on clothes. He would grab all color Dickies from Dan Steven's. Black Dickies was his favorite. He played them with flannels and his tan or black Timberlands. This was like the hustlers attire. Rod was right. Not only was most of the chicks in school paying attention to him, but Simone and Turquoise was all over him. Rod stayed on top of him and their designated place to meet up at was the chill spot. A coded knock on the door grabbed Malley's attention as he awaited Rod.

"Who is it?" Malley asked.

"It's me," spoke Rod. Malley looked through the peephole to make sure it was him. As he opened the door letting him in, he gave Rod a shake and hug once the door was closed.

"What's up ol' head?" he questioned.

"I'm good, everythin' cool?" he asked.

"Yeah, just waitin' on you. The duce is out and L.A. is blowin' my hitter up," he responded.

"I was tryin' to get with you asap but my people was dry for a minute. How much you got tucked youngin'?" asked Rod.

"I got four stacks and a few loose hundred," he replied.

"Alright, that's good. Make three different stashes; one for bail money, lawyer money and one in case you take a loss and gotta get back. That's how you stack, dig me?" Rod asked, after giving him game.

"Yeah, I got you," he answered. He could tell Rod was starting to dig his ghost outside of him being family but as a comrade of the game.

"I'ma be gone for 'bout two weeks," Rod said.

"Where you shootin' to?" he asked in suspense.

"I'ma breeze through the Bahamas and St. Lucia. I need you to maintain the duce and 55th Street. I just want you pickin' up doe. I got my other youngin's to handle the rest. When you pick up the doe, breeze through in somethin' tinted. When I get back graduation on me," said Rod.

"Yeah?" Malley asked surprisingly.

"Yeah, I got you," he promised.

"Oh, I ain't tell you the chicks luvin' me on the calm. They be breakin' their neck to speak to me, but I just be like what's up, or act like I don't even see 'em," said Malley.

"You learnin'. Keep it that way. Make 'em chase you. I'ma show you how to step your game up. I gotta go. It's four ounces in the bag. L.A. got access to more work if you need it. I'll get with you when I get back. If anybody asks where I'm at, tell 'em I'm layin' dead down North," Rod insisted.

"Got you," he replied.

Rod didn't want nobody to know that he was out of the city. He knew this would be a great opportunity for his rivals or would be robbers to try to make a move on his operation. Malley did what he was supposed to do. He grabbed the money off of the posts and dropped off on the posts. He did this every other day. As time went on, Malley was able to start taking care of the home front. His mom knew that he ain't have a job at the time, so he told her that Kaeem had got him one fixing roofs. He wasn't sure if his mom was convinced that the money he was earning came from fixing roofs, but it was no way that he could tell her that he was a drug dealer. The thought of him working legitimately made her somewhat happy, on top of going to school everyday.

CHAPTER 9

Friday came and Malley was feeling great. He had just counted $15,000 the night before. Even though it was Rod's money, it was the most money he had ever seen or counted at once. It made him feel like he was rich. Malley had $5,500 saved up and that was good to be only fifteen so in all actually he was ripping it. Malley felt good not being in position to wear the same gear to school back to back. Those days seemed to be over for him. It was time to get ready for school so he wiped the cold out of his eyes and jumped in the shower. He had "Big Payback" by E.P.M.D. knocking, while he focused on how he was going to step in school with his Sergio tech sweats, Airmax's and his Herring bone. He hopped out of the shower, dried off and got dressed, grabbing like $400 to play with. He double-checked himself before leaving to make sure he was intact. He pulled up in front of Grandma Goodies and ordered his usual. Grandma Goodies was a popular variety store down the street from Shoemaker that everybody went to in the mornings. Malley parked on Peach Street, entering school from the side entrance. As he imaged his vision was accurate. It was hard for the girls to keep their eyes off of him. Girls that never spoke to him a day in their lives, spoke this day. He began to feel himself just a little. On the inside he felt good. He didn't feel ashamed no more. He now had money in his pocket and he looked like money. Malley played the part of pretending like he didn't see his classmates checking him out. He carried on nonchalantly which brought his stock up immediately. From class to class he maintained the same poise until it was time for lunch. This was the moment he was waiting on, for the lunch bell to ring. Once it rang he dropped his books off in his locker and stepped in the lunchroom like he made it. He spotted Holly, a friend of his who was accompanied with Simone who was looking good as ever, but he couldn't let her see him sweat. His whole focus was to make her sweat him. She was only two people behind him in line.

"May I help you?" the clerk asked as Malley approached the counter.

"Yeah, let me get two cheese pretzels, two Tetley iced teas and a pack of Butter Crunch cookies," he said.

"Is that all?" asked the clerk.

"Yeah," he replied. Malley knew that the time was now. Despite him wanting her to sweat him, he needed to get in good company with her, so he figured he would pay for her girlfriend Holly's lunch, then pay for hers.

"Malley," Holly called, anticipating him to turn around.

"Damn, what's up Holly? I ain't know you was back there," he said, as he turned around, also placing his eyes on Simone.

"Yup, I'm here, Mr. playa, playa," she stated, with a smirk on her face.

"Why you say that?" he asked, never taking his eyes off of Simone.

"Yeah alright, keep playin' dumb then," she said, knowing he was trying to front in front of Simone because he was getting some money now.

"You trippin', but order what you want," he insisted.

"You sure in a good mood," she stated.

"That ain't 'bout nothin'. What you want sweetheart?" he stated to Holly, then questioned Simone.

"Excuse me?" she asked, a bit indignant.

"You heard me, what you want sweetheart?" he asked again, standing his ground.

"I'm good," Simone stated. Malley was aware that she was just trying to put up a defense. It was evident that she started to take a like into him. Her eyes spoke a thousand words and he was down to play her little game.

"Ay sexy don't do that to me. I'ma feel some type way," Malley said.

"I got my own money," she stated, in a sweet low voice.

"Let me handle that. It wouldn't be right if I don't pay for it," spoke Malley knowing she was just playing hard to get.

"You sure?" she replied, giving into his charm.

"Yeah, I got it," said Malley, pulling out a knot of money. Holly and Simone's eyes grew huge. He knew that he had to take control of the moment, so he paid for their things and began to leave. Simone kept her eyes locked on him as he exited the cafeteria. Everything played into his hands anyway as he never stayed all day on Fridays. He accomplished the first stage of making Simone want him even more. He tore down her resistance with that move. Holly was even at a loss for words. Simone started to bite on her thumb nail, wandering off into a place in her mind she could only fathom.

"Ay Holly, you gonna get at the bol for me?" Simone asked, very interested.

"You pulled your shovel out quick, huh?" said Holly, being smart.

"What are you talkin' about?" Simone questioned, playing dumb.

"Come on gold-digger," spoke Holly.

"Naw, he cute," Simone said, blushing.

"Yeah right, his money cute," Holly emphasized, insinuating that she knew Simone's angle.

"Holly, just holla at him for me," she replied with a slight sign of desperation across her face.

"Alright, I got you girl," Holly stated.

CHAPTER 10

On Malley's way home he made sure he called Kaeem to see what they were going to get into later. Kaeem was always with whatever what was on the agenda. No matter what they decided to do something was going to jump off, especially on a Friday night.

"Hello?" Kaeem answered.

"Yo, what's up. It's Mal," he said.

"What's goin' on?" Kaeem asked.

"Ain't nothin'. I'm tryin' go out tonight," stated Malley.

"Where you tryin' shoot to?" he questioned.

"We can spin down 40th Street," Malley mentioned.

"Yeah, I'm with that. Where you at right now?" Kaeem asked.

"On 48th & Girard at K.F.C. Y'all want somethin'?" he asked.

"Yeah, grab me some spicy and honey barbecue wings," spoke Kaeem.

"What Lil J' want?" he questioned.

"Some chicken tenders and widges," Lil J' stated in the background.

"Alright, we'll talk when I get there," said Malley, before hanging up.

A few knocks on the door took Lil J' and Kaeem out of their zone as they sat on the couch awaiting Malley to arrive with the food. Malley being a bit impatient decided to knock again after he didn't hear no answer.

"Who is it?" Kaeem questioned as he made his way to the door, peeking out the peephole.

"It's me, open the door," spoke Malley with bags of food in his hands.

"Damn, what took you so long?" Kaeem asked, opening the door, rubbing his stomach in circles.

"Yeah, I'm starvin' too death," said Lil J' putting his two cents in it.

"Man, I had to take care of somethin'. Where your miz?" he questioned, walking in the house. He needed to make sure his aunt was nowhere around.

"I don't know," Lil J' replied.

"Lets hit the basement," Malley stated, trying not to waste no time.

"Man, I'm hungry as shit. I ain't eat all day," spoke Kaeem.

"Shit, me too," Malley said.

"Alright, hold up. Let me grab somethin' real quick," Lil J' said.

"Man, come on Ka' the hell with Lil J, I'm tryin' eat," Malley spoke. Him or Kaeem wasn't going to wait for Lil J'. They proceeded down the basement to start knocking their food off.

"Man, I'm tryin' buss a grub too," said Lil J' wasting no time walking right behind them. They found their way onto the wrap-around leather sofa and began to politic as they ate. They could see all in Malley's actions that he was now getting to a couple dollars. The transition of seeing him with money now made them develop a small happiness for him. They didn't really like the fact that their cousin had to struggle more than them. At times Malley would catch Kaeem and Lil J' just nodding their heads without saying a word. He automatically knew that it was sort of a stamp of approval that his condition was changing. At that moment, what was understood didn't have to be explained. After he finished eating and making sure the money he had picked up earlier was straight, he decided to nod off so they could get ready for 40th Street.

As nightfall came, Kaeem and Lil J' woke Malley so they could crush the night. They were already dressed to impress and ready to leave. Malley stretched and yawned trying to gather his bearings. He brushed his teeth, washed his face, then they all made their exit. When they pulled up on 40th Street, it was jam packed in front of McDonalds and Burger King. It looked like the movies had just let out. Cars were parked and riding by with their music bumping. The chicks were everywhere making it hard to choose. This was definitely the scene to be on. Most of the crowd's eyes were glued on Malley, Lil J' and Kaeem as they rode by in the LSC. It was a few familiar faces that they recognized. Malley's main concern was to find a parking spot so they could get out and mingle. He had to drive around the block and park on 40th & Spruce across the street from Billy Bob's and the

Laundromat/arcade that stayed open all night. They hopped out and walked down to where everything was happening. Nothing but bad chicks were walking up and down the block. In fact, one walked right past Malley that he refused to let get away from him. She had an hour-glass shaped body, a walk out of this world and brown skinned, with a Toni Braxton hairstyle. Drop dead wasn't the word. She was a force to reckon with.

"Goddamn, she bad as shit," Kaeem said, tapping Malley's side. He was already in a trance of his own.

"I know. I'ma go right at her," he stated with confidence.

"Mal, that's a grown ass woman," said Kaeem.

"Yeah," Lil J' said speaking his mind. The fact of the matter was that the both of them was correct. She was grown and looked to be out of his league. She walked right across the street to McDonalds. Malley wasted no time following her into McDonalds. Kaeem was trying to convince him to fall back, but he paid him or Lil J' no mind. The only thing on his mind was to try to bag this chick. The fact that he was getting to a couple dollars now boasted his confidence. In all actuality he wasn't ready for her. He hopped right in her line, giving the customer behind her a few dollars to get in front of them. As she began to place her order, Malley decided to make his move.

"Hi you doin?" Malley asked, with a basic pick-up line. She turned around looking past him as if he didn't even exist. After she noticed that he was trying to come on to her, she finally spoke.

"Excuse me?" she asked.

"Damn sexy it's like that?" he questioned.

"Little boy, I know you ain't tryin' talk to me?" she questioned.

"Little boy? And yeah, what's wrong with that. That's a crime?" Malley asked, trying to fight her disapproval.

"Look you way too young, plus I have a brother your age," she replied. You could literally hear Lil J' and Kaeem in the background laughing. They tried to warn Malley but he had to learn on his own. She had on Louis Vuitton from head to toe. Malley started getting the feeling that he wasn't going to be able to pull her, but he kept trying anyway.

"Look, can I at least pay for your meal?" he questioned.

"I'm alright," she replied, opening up her alligator purse to pay for her food. She had at least twenty to thirty C-notes within it.

"What's your name though?" she asked.

"Malley, I'm from 62nd & Market." He spoke, trying to plant in her head hoping that would mean something being as though Market Street was known for producing a long line of bread winners.

"All that, huh? Well my name is Tasha," she said.

"If you don't mind me askin', how old are you?" he inquired.

"I'm 22. Look, I gotta go," she stated, grabbing her food and sauntering her sexy ass out of McDonalds. Kaeem and Lil J' continued to laugh. He didn't like what just happened but he had no choice but to suck it up and respect it. Kaeem brought his laughter to a stop and began to bring Malley up to speed to who she really was.

"Mal, you way out of your league. Her boyfriend gettin' it like Rod get it," Kaeem said, wanting that fact to sink into his head.

"Who her boyfriend?" Malley questioned.

"Ol' head bol from 49th Street," Kaeem stated.

"Damn, she got me fucked up, Ka. She tough as a muh'fucka. I'ma get that," Malley said, still not counting himself out.

"You trippin'," he replied, even though he respected his enthusiasm.

"Ka', I got money saved up," he spoke.

"It ain't like the bol money, he chewin' man," Kaeem reiterated, making a lot of sense.

"Yeah, you right. Lets get out of here. I gotta go pick this change up. I'ma drop y'all off," he said, giving into the reality of the situation.

CHAPTER 11

He dropped them off and went to check on the posts like he said he was going to do. As soon as he pulled up, the main young bol they had controlling the post, began to approach the whip with a black duffel bag. Malley signaled for him to get in. The young bol got in and they pulled off. He just wanted to go somewhere a little more secluded. He drove around the corner and parked. The youngin' handed him the duffel bag. When Malley opened it to peep the dough, a slight stench rose from the bag. It was the smell of blood money — $6,000 was enclosed. He zipped it back up then continued bussing it up with him. He explained to the youngin' that once he got down to a stack for him to beep him so he could bring some more work around to keep the operation running. The youngin' agreed and Malley pulled off so he could drop him back off on the block. As the car came to a stop, he gave Malley a pound and looked both ways before he got out of his whip. Malley drove off smoothly, while the smoke from the exhaust pipes vanished into thin air. After he made all of his rounds he finally made his way to the crib.

The next morning Malley awoke to the smell of bacon and eggs. As he cracked his door he could also smell fabric softener in the air. He figured his mom was washing clothes. Starving like a hostage he found himself going downstairs to the kitchen, where his breakfast awaited him on the table. As he suspected, his mom was washing clothes.

"Look who finally woke up," she said, folding clothes.

"Yeah, me, Kaeem and Lil J' went to the movies last night," he stated.

"Did y'all have a good time?" she asked.

"Yeah," he said, taking a bite of his bacon.

"How was school yesterday?" she inquired.

"It was alright. Ay mom I got a question?" he asked, getting off the subject.

"What is it?" she asked, sitting the laundry basket on the table.

"It's about this girl," he said.

"You ain't got nobody pregnant do you?" she questioned.

"Naw," he responded.

"Oh, because you got to watch these fast ass girls," she said, giving her input.

"Listen mom, I really took a liken into this girl," he said.

"What's her name?" she asked.

"Simone," he replied.

"Does she like you?" she asked.

"That's the thing, I don't know. How do I find out?" he questioned.

"First of all try spendin' some time with her. Look for signs, like the way she looks at you, or her moods when she's around you," she said, giving her son some sound advice.

"Alright, thanks," he said.

"Ain't no thanks. I see you got another pair of glasses, huh?" she questioned.

"Yeah. Mom we did three roofs last week," he replied, trying to lower her suspicion.

"How come your boss don't never drop you off sometimes?" she asked.

"Becuz he drops off other people, who live further than me. Mom I have a hundred towards this month's rent," he said.

"Malley, I love you. Your dad would have been proud of you," she stated.

"Mom, forget that coward," Malley said in anger.

"What you say boy? I bet not never hear you talk about him like that again. I mean that as long as I'm livin' on this earth," she replied in a stern manner.

"Mom, he left us in this situation. Men don't do that," Malley said, wanting to get his point across.

"That's still your father, no matter what. I'll talk to you later," she said, continuing to fold the clothes. Malley found himself returning back to his room, shaking his head. In his mind he couldn't believe that the love his mother had for his dad caused her to justify his actions. It had him a little twisted but he had to continue to focus on getting that money. Waiting for

Rod to get back seemed liked forever. In the little bit of time he was gone he began to step his game up. Malley was now sitting on $15,000 of his own and $30,000 of his cousin's money.

CHAPTER 12

When he went to school that Monday him and Simone locked eyes and she approached him instantly. He was kind of taken aback by her approach.

"What's up with me and you?" Simone asked boldly with no shame in her game awaiting his response.

"I don't know, you tell me," he replied.

"I'm not really never this aggressive but I see somethin' I want," she said.

"Oh, you a go-getta?" he asked.

"If that's what you call it," she stated.

Simone looked him up and down and walked away, leaving him at a loss for words. All she wanted to do was let him know that she was just as interested in him as he was in her. She invaded his mind all day in school. She had him chasing her and he knew he had to play his part, so he pulled up in front of Shoe in his LSC waiting for her. As soon as he spotted Simone and Holly walking down the steps, he hit the horn pulling up on the side of them. Simone was smiling from ear to ear as she listened to Malley trying to smooth talk her from his car. Holly was making faces at Malley but he really wasn't paying her any attention. This day his eyes were strictly for Simone and Simone only. She continued to walk playing hard to get. Her resistance turned him on even more. Game was on and he was up for the chase.

"So Simone can I take you home?" he asked.

"I'm right up the street," she said.

"I know, that's not what I asked you though," he replied.

"I guess so," she answered.

"You want me to drop you off to Holly?" he asked.

"No, I'm okay. You go ahead. I'll call you later," she said. Malley stopped the car and opened the door for her. You could see the jealously written across many faces of those out there. Malley pulled off playing "Out On A Limb" by Teena Marie, heading towards 52nd Street. Units of eyes stayed glued on his car, watching his right taillight blink as he turned the corner.

"So what was up with Holly?" he questioned.

"I don't know. I guess she was a lil' salty that you offered to take me home first," she replied.

"I ain't know Holly was into that," he said.

"Me either," Simone expressed, shrugging her shoulders.

"I see you catchin' feelin's," he stated.

"What? You trippin' boy," she said with a small giggle.

"Why you laughin', if I'm trippin'?" he asked.

"I can laugh. The last I checked this was a free country," Simone stated.

"Yeah, alright," he replied. He knew he had her where he wanted her. They both used to take sneak peeks at each other, so now it was all about making each other comfortable in each others presence. He couldn't help himself from admiring her beauty.

"Boy you better watch the road," she stated, smiling, showing the whites of her teeth.

"I got this, you hungry?" he inquired.

"Kind of," she said.

"Where you wanna go?" he asked.

"I do got a taste for some McDonalds," she responded.

"Mickey-dee's, huh?" he questioned.

"Yeah, some Mickey-dee's," she responded, smiling again. The chemistry was beyond apparent, the sparks were flying. The closest McDonalds was on 52nd & Chestnut and they were on 52nd & Girard, so that was a straight run, putting them there in ten minutes tops. Everybody and their mother was out on the Strip. This is what most called 52nd & Market. As they drove across Market Street heading towards Chestnut, merchants were everywhere attending to customers at their stands. Malley took faint glances at Olympian Sports Wear and The Jock Shop as if he wanted to pull over and buy some sneakers, but he kept afloat until he made his way into the McDonalds drive thru.

"Welcome to McDonalds. Can I take your order?" the cashier asked.

"Yeah, can I get a number 2, super sized and what you want?" Malley asked.

"You can get me the same thing," she stated.

"Two number twos," said Malley.

"Okay, you can drive around," the cashier spoke. Malley drove around to pay for and pick up their food. He took 52nd Street straight up to Parkside where Simone had lived. He wasn't sure if it was cool to drop her off at her house, so he stopped at the bus stop where the 52 ran. Simone looked at him like he was crazy when he pulled over.

"Boy, you can drop me off at my house. I live right there on Viola Street," she told him.

"Oh, I ain't know if it was cool or not," he replied honestly.

"Back up and make that right," Simone said, pointing to the narrow block which had a bunch of trees on it. He turned down the block and pulled up to her house. She lived a few houses away from the corner. A Getty gas station was right across the street from her house.

"Thanks Malley," she said, about to get out of the car.

"This ain't nothin'. I'ma call you later," he stated.

"I want you to meet somebody," she said.

"Meet who?" he asked.

"Nobody stupid, stop bein' paranoid. I'm just jokin'," Simone replied.

"You crazy, you know that?" he questioned.

"Umm-hmm, call me later," she said.

"Alright," Malley answered, driving off smoothly.

Pulling Simone was a major accomplishment for him. Kaeem couldn't even believe he bagged her, but he wasn't going to throw salt in the game. He took his hat off to him. All this did was make Malley want to go after Turquoise even harder now that he was kicking it with Simone. The angle was pretty much easier, being she was his God-sister babysitter. At this point he was kind of feeling himself. The money was pouring in, the chicks was loving him and his graduation was on the way. He felt untouchable, couldn't nobody tell him nothing but Rod. He was still away and out of all of his money. Malley never took a dime. Rod had put him on and the respect for him was of the utmost. As Malley sat on his bed counting some money his beeper went off. Once he saw the secret code he knew that Rod was back or close, so he quickly called the number back.

"Yo," Rod said, picking up on the first ring.

"What's up ol'head?" he asked.

"Ain't nothin'. Look, I just landed. Meet me at the chill spot in a half," Rod stated.

"Alright," he agreed.

"Make sure you bring that," Rod said speaking about the money. Although that was his cousin, it was business and drug money wasn't to be played with.

CHAPTER 13

He slid to the chill spot only to find out that Rod hadn't arrived yet. After a few minutes going by, he heard a key being placed in the lock. Rod walked through the door with his hoodie on.

"What's up? How was your trip?" Malley asked, happy to see him back.

"It was luvely," he responded.

"I see, look how dark you got," stated Malley.

"I'ma take you one day, that's my word. How much change you got?" he asked, wanting to get right down to business. He also wanted to see if he held it down while he was gone. It was all a big test to see where Malley's loyalty and determination was at.

"I got ten stacks," Malley replied. Rod rubbed his palms together seeming ready to count his bread.

"Damn lil-buddie, you was rippin' it, huh?" he asked, being rhetorical as he saw that he had his money straight.

"I'm just tryin' get it like you," he replied.

"Naw, get it more than me," Rod said, giving him inspiration.

"Right," Malley stated.

"You've been stackin'?" he questioned.

"No doubt," Malley answered.

"Alright. I told you graduation was on me, when I got back. When is it again?" he asked.

"June 26th," he answered.

"Alright, I got you covered," Rod reassured.

Malley filled Rod in with his progress with Simone and his attempt to lock Turquoise down. He couldn't stop him from cracking smiles. He was proud of his young bol. He began to see himself in Malley when he was a youth. He put Malley up to conduct a loyalty test with Simone. He told him to leave money around her and to send somebody to crack on her. He didn't want to send Kaeem or Lil J' because it would have been too obvious. Those were a couple ways to fill her out for the time being. Malley's mom wasn't aware yet that he was driving, so he was still flying under the radar. Rod embedded in his head to keep playing it low and stay loyal. He promised that only great things were to come and that he would be major one day. He was giving him the game on all levels making it almost impossible for anybody Malley's age to be on his level. This was going to make him irresistible from younger and older chicks. It seemed to be like Malley was on his way and Rod was going to make sure that he reached the top.

CHAPTER 14

After Rod left to handle some other business, picking up Simone and taking her to school is what he thought about. Turquoise even found her way on his mind. Simone was a bad chick, but Turquoise was the baddest chick in Shoe, so thoughts of taking her to prom was something he wanted to make a reality. As Simone was leaving her house Malley was just pulling up. He chose to pick her up early so they could go get some breakfast from Ace's Diner. Ace's was the go to spot in the mornings on 56th & Lancaster, even though Tony Boys kept 60th & Market packed in the mornings as well. Either spot would do. Simone got in the car planting a kiss on Malley's cheek. He tried to lean over and kiss her back but she moved her face away.

"Mmm-mm," she said.

"Good morning to you too," he stated, seeing that she wanted to play games early in the morning.

"Good things come to those who wait," she responded.

"Solid," he replied, driving off.

As he opened the door the smell of some good breakfast being cooked in Ace's smacked him and

Simone dead in their faces. All Malley could think about was how he was about to devour his usual. He wasted no time ordering a dish of scrambled eggs, home fries, grits and their famous toast. Simone chose a turkey egg and cheese sandwich with fried onions and green peppers. She also ordered an orange juice as Malley ordered a Welches Grape drink. They sat at the booth, ate and talked. Simone was beginning to really like him. She told Malley that she wanted him to meet her mom. He was kind of caught off guard by it being so early, but he could see she had other reservations. Simone was letting her mom know how good he treated her. In Malley's mind he wasn't ready to meet Simone's mom. He was ready to get in between Simone's legs. Plus Turquoise was well in the equation. Simone was a bit high maintenance so he gave her the nickname S or S-class, a high luxury class of a Mercedes. She smiled at the fact of him renaming her. His entire approach was different. Nobody never presented themselves to her like Malley was doing. She continued to blush, falling completely under his spell of so-called macking. Time had begun to escape them and school was about to start so they headed on their way to school. Malley dropped her off at the side entrance. She invited him to a kiss as he moved in with the speed of lightning, just to feel his lips against hers. As their lips parted she closed the door, heading towards the entrance. He nodded, feeling to himself that things were somewhat coming together. He parked up the street so the principal, or a nosey teacher wouldn't see him.

Kaeem and Malley had met up with each other in the hallway during third period. They were just up to their everyday shenanigans—cracking on chicks and ditching the NTA's during hall sweeps. Malley had taken it to another level. He was now bringing his work to school with him. He couldn't creep in the house during school hours everyday with the neighbors lurking, so he kept it with him. He really had to be on his p's and q's now. Kaeem kept tapping Malley to show him that Turquoise was coming up the hall and she was owning it. She gave Malley a come and get me look as she approached him.

"Hey, Malley. What's up? Kaeem told me you like me. I see you shy, huh?" she asked, pulling no punches.

"Not at all," he responded, looking at Kaeem as he was caught off guard.

"Yes you are. Look, here go my number, make use of it," Turquoise said as she grabbed his hand, writing her phone number on his palm. She winked at Kaeem and walked away switching her heart-shaped derriere. Malley looked at it, looked at Kaeem, then looked at his palm, nodding at the fact that he had bagged Turquoise. His next task was to get her in pocket. It was inevitable that he was going to get Turquoise, but Kaeem made it happen easier and quicker. Kaeem wanted to see his cousin shine. He was way beyond a selfish person. This was his way of showing him some love. The bell rang starting the next period. Students began to disperse through the hallways, making their way to their next class. Malley and Kaeem departed, vowing to meet up later. School was only a half a day so he was outside waiting for Simone like he told her he would be. He made sure he wiped Turquoise's number off of his palm before he met up with her. He couldn't get caught slipping this early in the game. He pulled alongside of her, bringing the car to a complete stop. She opened the door and got in. He had the Mary J. Blige's version of "Sweet Thing" playing on mellow pulling off turning up 52nd Street.

Regardless of Malley making it known that he wasn't ready to meet Simone's mom, she still manipulated the situation of him meeting her earlier than he wanted to. Ms. Maxine was sweeping the pavement as he arrived at her house. Now it was no way he could elude contact with Ms. Maxine and Simone knew this in the back of her mind. She pointed at a parking spot for him to pull into. He pulled in the parking spot and turned the car off. Ms. Maxine was a cool, or what most would call a mom who was down to earth. With the car turned off and Malley glancing at Ms. Maxine who continued to sweep, keeping her eyes glued on the car, Malley still had no idea that this woman staring at them was Simone's mom and on top of it all he was about to meet her. Simone got out of the car giving her mom a hug. Malley followed only to be ambushed by Simone's sneaky tactic to introduce him to her mother. For Ms. Maxine to be her age, she was a hot red bone who could give a lot of young girls a run for their money. The jeans she had on were fitting her like a glove. Simone surely had inherited her mother's beauty and body.

"How are you? I am Simone's mother. My name is Ms. Maxine," she stated, being polite.

"Hi, my name is Jamal, but most call me Malley," he humbly said, unable to believe how sexy her mother was. She could of literally passed for her older sister. Ms. Maxine was a product of the game. She came up in the Black Mafia era, so she had been around and dealt with some major players in the city. She even witnessed the J.B.M. era take off and had her hands on one of their players also. She pretty much was used to the fast lane. She loved the rush of being whined and dined, being taken to five star restaurants, presidential hotel suites, driving in luxury cars, being draped in diamonds, and covered in minks. You name it, this is what she loved. These high rollers made Atlantic City and New York her second home. And although these players run would always come to an end, rather it being jail, or death, she always sought out the next up and coming player as the game stayed the same. Even the women who played in this game were stern when it came to their agenda. Some women would have babies by these players in the game, so they could always be attached to them, or some just wanted to be seen with them, resorting back to the allure of it. These types of women were known as gold diggers, or black widows. Ms. Maxine invited Malley inside. While the two got acquainted, Simone went in the kitchen to get Malley something to drink.

"Okay Malley, the charmer, who's been charmin' my baby," Ms. Maxine said, opening up a line of dialogue between him and her.

"Malley the charmer, huh?" he responded back.

"How old are you?" Ms. Maxine asked.

"Fifteen," he responded.

"Where do you live?" Ms. Maxine asked.

"I'm from Summer Street projects, but I play up 62nd & Market," Malley answered.

"You got a lot goin' on to be fifteen. Where do you work at?" she inquired.

"Mom, you all up in his business," Simone said, returning from the kitchen with two sodas.

"It's okay. I work for a roofin' company," he replied, answering Ms. Maxine's question.

"Look, Malley I've seen it all and done it all," she said, cutting him off, hinting at a much bigger picture.

"Seriously, I work for a roofin' company," Malley stated, trying to convince her, which seemed to not be working.

"I know you in the game. It's not my business, just be careful. My business is my daughter. Whatever you do, don't hurt her. She really like you," Ms. Maxine expressed to him.

"You ain't gotta worry about that. I like her too, Ms. Maxine," he responded.

"Malley did y'all do it yet?" she asked, going straight for the jugular.

"Huh, what?" he asked, taken aback. He would of never expected Ms. Maxine to be so forward with him. In a way he didn't mind it because it showed him that she's understanding.

"Don't play dumb, you heard me the first time," she replied, in a joking manner.

"Mom . . .," Simone spat, being a little embarrassed by her mother's boldness.

"What? Ain't no mom. When that day come make sure y'all use protection. She has to finish school, no exceptions," she said, making him fully aware.

"I respect that," he replied.

"Alright then we have an understandin'," she said.

"No doubt," he stated, taking a sip of his soda, trying to hide his nervousness.

"It was nice meetin' you," Ms. Maxine stated, walking up the stairs.

"You too," he replied back.

"My mom is crazy ain't she?" Simone questioned.

"She about her work. But I like how you put this together," he stated.

"What?" she responded with a smile on her face, playing dumb. She knew what she had done.

"Yeah, alright. Look I gotta go, but I'ma call you later," he replied.

"You better," she said leaning in to give him a kiss. They locked lips, tasting the sweetness of each others tongues. They parted and she stood in the doorway watching him get in the car and drive off.

CHAPTER 15

As usual the weekend had came fast once again. Malley called Kaeem and Lil J' to see what they were going to get into.

"Hello?" Lil J' answered.

"Yo, what's up?" Malley asked.

"Ain't nothin'. What's with you?" Lil J' questioned.

"I just got off the horn with Turquoise," he replied.

"Yeah, what she talkin' about?" he asked.

"A bunch of nothin'," Malley responded, playing it down.

"I can't tell. I hear she wanna break you." Lil J' insinuated that she wanted to have sex with him.

"Yeah, she did say she was tryin' go out tonight," he stated.

"You goin' to take her out? You know she feelin' you?" Lil J' said, trying to pump him up.

"She did say she got some girlfriends. I'ma see if we all can go out," Malley insisted.

"Oh, I'm with that. Where we goin' shoot to?" Lil J' questioned.

"I don't know. We can hit the movies," Malley said.

"Man, I'm tired of the 40th Street," Lil J' stated.

"Naw, 69th Street," Malley said.

"Alright, the nine will work," Lil J' replied.

"Look, I'ma call her and put her on point. Put Ka' on point when he come in," Malley said.

"Alright, later," Lil J' said.

Malley wasted no time calling Turquoise. They had been calling each other back and forth ever since she gave him the number. Turquoise laid across her bed in her pink and black t-shirt and panties, enjoying the sound of Malley's sexy voice as he smooth talked her. His main objective was to set up a nice get together between her, her girlfriends and him and his cousins. She was into the whole thing, so getting her friends to agree wasn't going to be a problem. Whatever she thought was cool to do they thought was cool to do. This is the type of influence she had on them. They put together a dinner and movie night at the United Artist Theater up 69th Street. Turquoise lived between 53rd & 54th of Montgomery Avenue. All up and down Wynnefield was some bad chicks. After he secured everything with her, he hung up so he could meet up with Rod.

Malley went to the chill spot only to see his old head already waiting for him. His henchmen stayed in the cut with their 9 millimeters already drawn in case some would-be robbers tried to rob the chill spot and a shoot-out ensured. He gave Rod a hug upon entering the house.

"What's up youngin'?" Rod questioned.

"Man . . . these chicks is on my top. They feelin' my style. That's what's up," Malley stated, shaking his head as he flopped on the couch biting into an apple.

"I guess so. You've been taught by the best," Rod said, acknowledging his work.

"I feel you ol'head," Malley replied.

"You gotta be in it to win it youngin'. You're doin' good, but this shit is about a purpose. If you're cool now, get out the game. You ain't got no cases and you ain't hot," Rod emphasized, as he saw that Malley was beginning to get sucked in the thrill of it. Malley's main goal was to accumulate enough money to make sure he was able to go to school up to par. He was now beyond that goal and now it was a choice that had to be made.

"I know, but look at all the things you got," Malley said.

"What the fuck, you ain't hear nothin' I just said? I'm in too deep. I been past my goal. The only way out for me is death. I'm in bed with some heavy weights," spoke Rod who had seemed to be stressed out. He held back the fact that he was getting his shipments from the Colombians.

"You said I was goin' to be major someday," he replied.

"I wasn't just speakin' in terms of the game. This game don't love, or give a fuck about you. Sixty-second Street, 52nd Street, Shoe and them chicks is gonna be here if we're dead or alive. Reach your goal and breeze. I'm schoolin' you only because you're family. These bitches is on me because I got doe. I'm drivin' fat whips and I throw that shit on. That's why, this go, they go." Rod continued to make the ills of the game as vivid as possible to him. This more in-depth insight broke down why Rod maneuvered the way he did.

"I'm gonna do some deep thinkin'," Malley stated, respecting everything he just laid on him.

"Yeah, you do that," he spoke.

"Oh, yeah I'm takin' Turquoise out tonight," Malley said.

"Yeah, well what's up with Simone?" he asked.

"She alright, I'm just feelin' her too," he stated, acknowledging that he had a thing for the both of them.

"Outer beauty definitely count, but don't underestimate the inner beauty. Turquoise might be badder than Simone, but Simone might want you for you. Not sayin' that's what's goin' on, but you gotta size them up," he said, dropping jewels on him left and right.

"Got you," Malley responded, knowing that he had to get on top of his job.

"How much the post do last night?" Rod inquired after stating his peace. This was the real reason they met up at the chill spot in the first place.

"It did three stacks," he answered, watching Rod nod his head as if this was an accomplishment. It was no telling what Larry Gunther or Bobby Cool's brought in.

"After the graduation, I'm takin' you on a trip. I'ma show you some other things in life, but don't forget nothin' we talked about today," he said, wanting to make sure his message got across.

"Alright, I'm about to pull up," Malley said.

"Alright, make sure you hit me over the weekend," Rod stated.

"No doubt," he answered, giving him a handshake, then leaving.

CHAPTER 16

As it got later on in the day, Malley, Lil J' and Kaeem stopped at the Green store on 58th & Baltimore that sold some killer weed. They picked up two dimes in case Turquoise and her girlfriends wanted to smoke. They made sure they at least grabbed a box of blunts in their travels. Malley drove to 52nd & Baltimore then took 52nd Street straight up to 52nd & Lancaster. He turned there because he didn't want Simone to see him drive through. He took the long way around having to cross the bridge to Wynnefield. He was thinking better safe than sorry. As they turned on Montgomery Avenue Turquoise and her girlfriends stood in front of her house looking sexier than ever. Malley pulled up, stopping in front of them. He rolled his window down and leaned up with his right hand gripped over the steering wheel. "Paid N Full" by Eric B and Rakim was playing in the background as he spoke over the music. Kaeem and Lil J' sat back playing their part.

"Yo, what's up? Y'all ready?" Malley asked her.

"Yeah boy we ready. Look my peoples is gone for the weekend. Y'all wanna spend the night?" Turquoise asked, trying to put things in place. Malley turned around looking at Kaeem and Lil J' checking their temperature. They wasted no time in agreeing to the hook up. He gave her the nod and in return she put her girlfriends on point.

"Let me get my jacket," she said, running in the house to get it. She came right back out and they all hopped in the car.

At the last minute Malley changed his mind, choosing to hit The Capital instead of 69th Street. The entire 52nd Street was lit up. The Capital was a popular movie theater in the hood that always drew a lot of attention. The release of "New Jack City" brought out crowds of players and arm candy from all over. People driving by in their cars couldn't even deny the ambience that the marquee of the sign brought. Security was a bit tight due to the controversy surrounded around the movie. The cops made sure their presence was felt as they patrolled up and down the strip. A lot of crews were playing hard. The previews of "New Jack City" had every aspiring drug dealer wanting to be Nino Brown. Turquoise walked next to Malley as they made their way to the ticket booth, while Shanda and Sonya stayed next to Kaeem and Lil J'. Malley slid the ticket conductor a few extra dollars as they really needed an adult to get in. The ticket conductor gave them the tickets and they entered without any problems. They walked straight to the concession stand, ordered some food, then went into the theater. The movie was just starting. Ice-T was chasing Pookey and Nino, and G-Money was plotting on taking over The Carter. Everyone sat next to each other. Lil J' and Kaeem felt good being around some bad chicks and Turquoise was all up on Malley like they had already made things official.

"Ay Malley, you know I'm feelin' you like that," Turquoise stated very clearly.

"Oh, yeah?" he answered.

"Yeah. I like how you hold it down," she replied.

"I try," he responded, letting her think that her little game she slid in went over his head. Her mom also dealt with some high rollers. Except the players she was involved with, stayed on the road using stolen credit cards and checks. Busting plastic was their twist. You could see the fast lane all within her character and Malley was attracted to it. The last scene of the movie was coming on where Nino Brown was walking down the courthouse stairs and the old man was upset about the fact of him beating the case. This was where he took justice in his own hands. He pulled out a gun, shot Nino Brown in the chest, killing him. "For The Love of Money" by Queen Latifah played as the credits started to roll and patrons began to disperse. They tried to leave with the first weave because somebody always got shot during the let out of a major movie or event. Malley parked right on Stiles Street for easy access. As they all got in the car, Kaeem asked if the girls smoked weed.

"Yeah, we get down," Shanda responded.

"We goin' spark somethin'. I got a duckie spot behind the Man Music Center," Malley stated, driving off.

"I'm with that," said Turquoise. Malley pulled over underneath a tree. This was the perfect spot where they could blaze up at. Kaeem sparked up, immediately taking a deep tote. Lil J' sparked up the next one, putting the blunts in rotation. The smell of the killer weed began to fill the car. When Lil J' passed the blunt to Turquoise she took a deep pull, holding it in like a pro. She turned it upside down giving Malley a shotgun. He inhaled as much as he could before coughing most of it back out. You could hear the snickers from everybody at the fact of him being unable to handle it. He didn't smoke weed. That was really Lil J' and Kaeem's thing. His Aunt Rita stayed smoking on the weekends and they used to steal the roaches from out of her ashtray and smoke them. Malley's eyes watered as he continued to cough. Shanda and Sonya couldn't wait for the weed to hit them. Turquoise was unable to keep her hands and lips off of Malley. He sat back relaxing, letting the weed marinate, while Turquoise's hands found their way into his lap.

"Can't wait to get to your spot," he said, getting turned on by how Turquoise was massaging his manhood with one hand and sticking her tongue in his ear at the same time.

"Patience is a virtue," she replied.

"Where J' and Ka gonna sleep?" he asked, feeling himself grow in his pants.

"Don't you mean smash?" she asked, whispering in his ear.

"Yeah," he replied, completely turned on.

"One of them can sleep in the basement and one of them can take my room," she answered.

"Where we gonna be at?" he questioned Turquoise.

"Damn, y'all just makin' us do it, where y'all want us to do it at, huh?" Shanda asked, interrupting them both, wanting to know where was their say so in the matter.

"Yeah, listen to y'all," spoke Sonya. Kaeem and Lil J' ain't say a word. They kept on smoking. They ain't care where, or how they was going to get some as long as they got some.

"Anyway, like I was about to say, we can use my mom bedroom," Turquoise reiterated.

Kaeem fanned his hand in front of his face trying to thin out the clouds of smoke that the blunts had produced. Every time one blunt came around, another one was being passed and lit. Lil J' looked as if he wanted the windows rolled down, but he couldn't let the chicks see him sweat when they weren't even complaining. It was contact galore and their eyes were burning. After sitting there and everybody looking at each other just stuck, Kaeem snapped out of the trance they were in, realizing that they were high as a light bill.

"Yo, Mal, come on we out," he said sluggishly.

"Huh, oh yeah we out, we out," he said, coming back to his senses. Lil J' was comatose as well. Malley rolled the windows down watching the smoke evaporate within the air. He ran his palm over his face, getting himself together. Turquoise, Shanda and Sonya's eyes were all chinked and they looked sexier than ever. They were mangled too. They didn't care they were one with the moment. They were now ready to get piped down. Malley didn't want to drive back across Parkside, so he took the back road to get to Wynnefield quicker. He couldn't wait to get to Turquoise's and relax. Getting in her panties was his only task.

CHAPTER 17

They arrived there and everything was on point. Kaeem and Lil J' went their way for the night with Shanda and Sonya and Malley and Turquoise went theirs.

Turquoise dimmed the lights as they entered the room, escorting him right to the bed. It seemed like this procedure was all so familiar, being she went right to her mother's jasmine scented candles that she kept on the nightstand and lit them. The aroma was complimenting the moment, making it a more comfortable environment. The unpredictability of Turquoise was turning Malley on even more. He laid across the bed, anticipating what was to come next. Turquoise turned on "Seems Like Your Ready" by R-Kelly, making her way over to him. She got on the bed and straddled him. He licked his lips as she moved in, placing her lips on his. He opened his mouth embracing her French kiss, pretending to know more than he knew. She pulled back, wiping the hair from in front of her face.

"You got a condom?" she asked, ready to further her naughtiness.

"Naw," he answered.

"Hold up, let me look in my mom's drawer," she said, only to speed up the process. Malley's mind was all over the place. All he was concerned about was knocking her off. Without hesitation she returned with a condom, waving it in the air, before giving it to him. She stripped down to her red and black panties, then down to her pretty nakedness. Turquoise climbed on the bed, straddling him again.

"Damn, you bad," he stated, looking at her flawless body.

"Malley, I want some. Can I have some?" she asked in a low tone with lust filling her eyes.

"Yeah," he answered, finding his breathing getting heavier and heart beating faster. Turquoise took his hands, running them over her erect brown nipples, which stood at attention on her succulent breasts. Making things spicier, she guided his hands down between her v-shaped peach, that was dripping of her sweet juices. This drove Malley crazy. Unable to take it anymore, he opened the condom and slid it on. His boxers ended up on the floor and she ended up on her back, with her legs gapped wide open. He inserted himself into her tight orifice and stroked back and forth. Turquoise began to dig her nails into his arms and back as he went deeper with faster strokes.

"Oh, Malley, boy you're in my stomach," Turquoise moaned, now feeling the full impact of his manhood. He kept quiet, continuing to pump her. The more he pumped her, the more wetter she became. The feeling of her wet tight love tunnel forced him to sigh as he could tell he was about to orgasm.

"Sss . . ." He hissed at how good she felt to him and how juicy she was getting. He could feel his climax building. He made it his job to imitate the moves he saw some porn star doing to Vanessa Del Rio in one of her movies. The guy was punishing her, she was literally begging for mercy. This is where he got his fast and hard swirling strokes from. The momentum caused Turquoise's moans to grow louder.

"Oh, shit I can't take it. Oooh . . . I'm cummin'," she cried out, letting herself glaze all over him. Now becoming sopping wet he could no longer fight back his urge to let go.

"Shit, I'm 'bout to nut," he blurted out, unable to keep his body from contorting. His lower body jerked until he came to a complete stop. He paused for a few seconds, pulled out, then rolled over looking at Turquoise. He was kind of blown away at how good her shot was. She was spent as well. They both laid there in awe.

"Boy your pipe game is like that. I need some weed," she said, giving him his props.

"Damn, the condom busted," he said after he looked down, noticing that the rim was rolled back and the remaining of the condom was tangled up. This is what he didn't' want, or need to happen.

"What, you came in me? How you do that?" she asked concerned.

"Shit, I don't know," he replied, not knowing what to think.

"You better not get me pregnant. My mom is gonna kill us," she stated.

"You cool, you ain't gonna get knocked up," he said, only to calm him and her down. All sorts of things started to travel through his mind. He hoped that she didn't poke a hole in the condom. He knew that she was a slick chick, but all in all, he was just glad he hit. They both were worn out and fell asleep in each others arms.

CHAPTER 18

Malley awoke to the sound of birds chirping. Turquoise's body still laid against his and the sight of waking up to her was pleasing. He ran his fingers through her silky air, amazed by her. She cracked a smile before opening her eyes.

Hey babe," she spoke in a low manner.

"Oh, you just gonna hit me with the mornin' breath?" Malley said, being sarcastic.

"Boy, my breath don't stink," Turquoise stated, pinching him in his side.

"Ouch, I was only playin', you good," he said, cleaning up his statement.

"You hungry? Want some breakfast?" Turquoise asked, wanting to pamper him as she laid her head on his chest.

"Yeah, I can bust a grub right now," he responded, running his fingers back through her hair.

"Alright, I got you." She gave him a peck on the lips then got up. He watched her walk off, pulling her wedged panties out of her ass, shaking his head. He took a deep breath, put his arms behind his head, then crossed his feet.

Turquoise threw on some more clothing and went to check up on her girlfriends. Little did she know that they were already awake and on the prowl to getting breakfast ready.

"Damn, y'all up bright and early," Turquoise said as Shanda and Sonya was invading the refrigerator, getting ready to make breakfast.

"Well good mornin' to you too," Shanda replied.

"Umm-hmm, yeah good mornin'," Sonya said, being smart.

"I'm not even gonna feed into both of you hoes," Turquoise responded.

"Anyway, what's up with Malley? He put his thing down?" Shanda asked, being nosey as she was cracking the eggs in the pan.

"Girl . . . he tore this thing up," Turquoise replied, without any doubts in his performance.

"What . . . he got a big thing?" questioned Sonya.

"He packin', plus he thoro and gettin' to a dollar," Turquoise said, helping to separate the bacon.

"Turquoise, that's all you think about," spoke Shanda.

"That's a lie. I think about dick too," she stated.

"Dick and dollars, dick and dollars," Sonya said, teasing her.

"Yeah, okay," Turquoise intervened, defending herself.

"You're a whore," said Sonya, with a smile on her face playing with Turquoise.

"F-you winch, you act like you're the only one who kept their coochie closed last night," Turquoise stated, trying to get her back.

"I wish I would of, with his little ass wee-wee," Sonya spoke.

"What, he got a little dick?" asked Turquoise.

"I was so mad last night. Don't hook me up no more with nobody that got a little thing, or don't know how to do it," spoke Sonya, getting her point across.

"Well, I'm glad Kaeem knew what he was doin'. Lets just say he hit it right," said Shanda, giving Turquoise a high five, making fun of Sonya.

The smell of breakfast being cooked traveled throughout the house, finding its way to Malley, Kaeem and Lil J'. Malley went to go check on his boys after encountering a wild night. He wanted to see if they shared in the same excitement. Kaeem was getting himself together when Malley walked into Turquoise's room.

"Yo, what's up Ka?" Malley asked.

"Ain't nothin', shorty wild man," he stated, with a smirk.

"Yeah?" he asked.

"Yeah, man Shanda's an animal. She chewed me up and all," Kaeem replied.

"Turquoise a beast too. What's up with Lil J'?" Malley asked, but before Kaeem got a chance to answer he came in the room.

"Yo, what's up with y'all?" Lil J' questioned.

"Ain't nothin', we chillin'," said Kaeem.

"What happened with you and Sonya?" Malley inquired.

"Man . . . I gave her the blues," Lil J' said short and quick not sounding like he was confident about how things turned out between him and Sonya.

"That's what I'm talkin' 'bout," Kaeem replied.

"Okay player," Malley said, trying to indirectly build back his confidence. He had already heard Sonya telling Shanda and Turquoise earlier, about how Lil J' was lacking in the man department. They were pretty much playing him about the whole ordeal as he was unable to satisfy Sonya.

CHAPTER 19

After making their way downstairs and eating breakfast, Malley dropped Lil J and Kaeem off on 62nd Street. Rod had beeped him, leaving the code for him to meet him at the chill spot. Rod awaited him as he knocked three times before letting him in. Malley was somewhat tired, but the adrenaline of getting money had him on the go.

What's up, youngin'?" Rod questioned, opening the door.

"This money," he said, pointing to a bag he had in his left hand.

"That's what I wanna hear. We gotta bag up and count some bread," he stated.

"We gotta bag up?" he asked.

"Yeah, lil Reek was lackin' and got pickled," said Rod.

"How much we bagin' up?" questioned Malley.

"We goin' count like twenty and bang up like a brick. We should at least be able to bang up nine ounces by 4:00 p.m. It's 10:00 a.m. now, hand me the scale and razors," Rod asked, looking at his watch.

"Alright," Malley said, getting the scale and razors out of the top drawer. He was going to burn the tips while Rod bagged up.

"So, what's up with you?" he asked.

"Ain't nothin', you know I bussed Turquoise last night," Malley said, wanting to let his old head know.

"The young jawn from Wynnefield?" he asked.

"Yup and her shot like that," he stated.

"Okay, youngin', I told you that it was a matter of time," Rod reiterated.

"But dig this, I bussed in her," Malley informed him.

"You ain't strap up?" he questioned, stopping in his tracks of chopping the coke.

"The joint popped," he told him.

"So what she say?" he asked, curious.

"She hope she don't get pregnant," he responded.

Rod inquired about Simone and if she knew about him and Turquoise. Malley let him know that she saw them talking, but didn't know that they had sex. It wasn't like she pursued him about their interaction, so he deemed himself to be in the clear. Even after hitting Turquoise before Simone, his emotions for her never went anywhere, they were just in two different places now. He respected Simone because she didn't let him hit so fast and then he also respected Turquoise because she let him hit, he enjoyed the best of both worlds. Rod did tell him that he should of gave Turquoise more time to get to know him, if he was trying to make her his girl, but it was a little too late for that. Everything replayed in his mind; from meeting her, to doing their thing, to meeting Simone and her mom. Malley was a young bol and he wasn't aware of chicks who had ulterior motives for drug dealers. All of this attention was fairly new to him. At this point he was just along for the ride, but Rod kept turning him on to different facets of the game. He wanted him as sharp as possible, because nobody was exempt from the trial and error that came along with life. With only a week left to graduate, Rod promised to take him to get a tailor made suit from Vizuris and some shoes from Bruttino's. Malley and Rod ended up finishing around 4:20 p.m. When he got home he was exhausted, but he made it his business to call Simone before he fell asleep.

"Hello?" Simone answered.

"What's up S'?" he asked.

"What?! What do you want?" she said in an angry tone.

"What's wrong?" he questioned, concerned.

"Look don't call me that. As a matter of fact, don't call, or say shit to me in school, call that bitch!" she told him.

"What are you talkin' about?" he asked.

"Don't play dumb, I'm talkin' about that bitch Turquoise. You got time for her, huh?" she stated, then questioned.

"You trippin'," Malley said.

"Trippin' my ass, my sources don't lie," Simone indicated.

"They're feedin' you some bullshit," he said, trying to get out of the argument.

"Stop lyin' boy. You're caught, you was at the Capital with the bitch on Friday," Simone stated firmly.

"Yeah, me, Ka' and J went," Malley stated in his defense.

"Yeah right, you're diggin' yourself a deeper hole. They seen y'all get out the car with them bitches. I thought you was tryna build somethin', but I see you ain't shit either," Simone said, slamming the phone down.

Malley couldn't believe that she hung up on him, leaving him listening to the dial tone. He knew he had screwed up. It didn't even matter which one of her friends seen him, the fact was that they seen him.

"Damn, I'm busted," he said to himself, looking at the phone. Before she didn't think of anything but now she believed they had a thing for each other, even with little evidence.

CHAPTER 20

Monday came and the first chance he got to see Simone was in the lunchroom and as he locked eyes with her, she rolled her eyes at him. Anger was written all across her face. Turquoise found her way over to Malley flirting with him. He decided to flirt back just trying to make Simone jealous. If anything this would have been a Parkside and Wynnefield rivalry as neither neighborhood never got along with each other.

"What she lookin' at?" said Turquoise being spiteful.

"Come on we out," he told her, trying to avoid an accident waiting to happen.

"Come here Malley! You betta not leave with that bitch!" Simone said loudly, wanting Turquoise to know that she felt the vibes. Of course, she was still mad at him but the cat fighting had begun.

"What did you say?" Turquoise replied.

"You heard what I said," Simone stated grabbing the back post of her right earring, ready to fight.

"Yo, y'all trippin', chill," Malley said, intervening. He placed his arms between the two of them creating a wedge. They were ready to lock on to each other like pit bulls.

"I'll kick her ass," stated Turquoise, trying to point over him, to put her hands in Simone's face.

"No you won't bitch! I'm from Parkside!" Simone yelled back without fear.

"Simone go 'head," Malley said, letting them both loose.

"Boy ain't no go 'head, it's because of you anyway that this bitch goin' get her ass kicked." Simone spoke with an evil look on her face. Her arms were folded across her chest with her right foot tapping the ground.

"Turquoise spin off. I'ma holla at you later. Simone come on. I'ma take you home," Malley said, trying to defuse the situation.

"No, you're not," Simone said, not wanting to be bothered.

"I'ma take you home," he insisted.

"Get off of me, don't touch me," stated Simone.

"Come here, let me explain," he tried to plead.

"No, don't touch me," she repeated, standing her ground.

"S you know I fuck with you like that," said Malley trying to turn his charm on.

"You ain't actin' like it messin' with that trash. You hurt me boy, give me one reason why I should consider givin' you another chance?" she questioned.

"Because don't no female make me feel how you make me feel. Take that frown off of your face. You're too pretty for that," Malley said smoothly, reaching for it. She instantly pulled her face away from his hands, not even slightly convinced by his fly talk. She got up and left in silence. Malley was left standing there in thought. The first thing that replayed in his head was the words of Simone's mother; "My business is my daughter, whatever you do, don't hurt her, she really likes you." His next step was to figure out how he was going to make things right.

The next few days the hood was on fire. You couldn't turn a corner without seeing unmark vehicles waiting and plotting to catch a dealer making a sell. Lee and Maclain were known as the jeep boys, or jump-out's. They were famous for jumping out their Bronco, Cherokee, or gold Volvo. The corner boys knew if they were caught by them selling drugs, they were going for a ride way past Cityline Avenue and they knew they were walking back with empty pockets. Between 55th & Pine and 61st & Thompson it was no telling which district were more corrupt. Both departments stayed harassing the Jamaican's who sold weed from 63rd & Market to Hirst Street. When they raided them, they would lay them face down on the ground, take most of their money and process them with the remaining weed they found. Rod never had any problems with the Jamaican's because they sold weed and he sold coke. Plus they would hit him off with some good ganja from time to time.

CHAPTER 21

All week seemed to be dragging since his argument with Simone. Despite the fact that he was graduating, he just couldn't stop thinking about her. The day had come and he ended up oversleeping.

"Malley, get up," stated his mother.

"Huh, in a minute," he replied half asleep.

"In a minute my ass! Boy, it's 9:05 a.m.," she emphasized.

"Alright mom, I'm up," he stated as he got up off of his bed, wiping the cold out of his eyes. He was already running late so he had to hit the shower quickly.

"Jamal, it's ten after," his mother yelled in the distance. But by this time, he was already getting dressed.

"I'm comin'. Give me a minute," he responded.

"Boy we're going to be late. We have to catch the 31 and the El," she stated. He raced downstairs dressed to impress.

"Come on, I'm already, we're drivin'," Malley spoke.

"You're driving where?" she questioned, looking at him as if he lost his mind.

"We drivin' to the graduation," he assured.

"Boy, where you get a car? I know you ain't bringing no drugs into my house?" she questioned.

"I work remember?" he responded, trying to lower her suspicion.

"How the hell you get a car? Look at your suit. Boy, you must really think I'ma damn idiot. Ain't no roofing job pay for them shoes on your feet," she said, not buying his story one bit.

"Mom I'm not tryin' to argue," he said.

"If you got any drugs in my house, you better get them out of here. You don't need that life. The jails, or graveyards will hold you. Look at your uncle," she stated, beginning to preach.

"Mom, can we leave? We late as it is. It's twenty after," Malley said, trying to push the issue.

"I'm not finished with you. And don't be driving all fast and playing all that hee-bop-bee-bop stuff either," she said, finally giving in.

"Alright mom," he replied.

"Ain't no alright mom. I laid on that table in labor for fifteen hours," she said, getting her point across.

From the way out the door, to getting in the car to all the way to Drexel University, she made sure she gave him an earful. He was kind of annoyed, but at the same time he knew she was just showing him her motherly love. And he just wanted to make her happy by graduating. The security guard stood at the entrance directing each patron to where the graduation were being held. Malley drove around the corner to the auditorium. The parking spots were limited but he was able to find one still vacant. After he parked, him and his mother had approached the auditorium as quickly as possible, putting on his cap and gown. Unfortunately, the worst case scenario had happened. The graduation was almost over. Malley stepped in the building cleaner than the board of health and of course all eyes were on him. Turquoise was stationed on one side so was Simone. Malley felt it but today was his day. "End of the Road" by Boyz II Men was coming to an end, while the entire auditorium sang along with each lyric, waving their hands from side to side. It had turned into a mini concert. The guess speaker began to speak as the song went off.

"Congratulations! I want to announce that the class of 1991-1992 has officially graduated," stated the guest speaker. The auditorium went into an uproar with cheers followed by each graduate throwing their caps in the air. The boys had on red caps and gowns as the girls had on all white. Red and white caps soared throughout the air. Malley turned around only to see his mother clapping with appreciation across her face. As he went to embrace her, a tear dropped out of her eye. For the first time in a long while he witnessed his mother's happiness.

"Son, I'm so proud of you, congratulations. I knew you could do it," she stated emotionally enjoying the moment. He didn't hear his mother talk like that since he graduated from elementary school.

Everyone began to depart. The dinner dance was being held at the Wynne-Plaza in Wynnefield, but most were heading up Roosevelt Boulevard to eat. It was some time before the festivities were to start. Rod had came over to show some love. His aunt Rita and grandmother also came over to support as well. The only thing on his mind was going to Red Lobster and eating. Most of his fellow graduates met up with him at the restaurant. The dishes were looking mighty delicious; jumbo butterfly shrimp, Alaskan snow crabs, lobster, you name it. Rod had something to do, so Malley and the rest of the family went to enjoy the day. Malley sat back in the chair stuffed, just sitting back talking about old times and how his grandfather was someone he wished was still alive to see his accomplishment. As time wound down, getting closer to the dinner dance, Malley wanted to get back and take care of a few things. He dropped his mom off, then went to get with Ka' and Lil J'.

"What's up?" Malley asked, with a smile on his face.

"Ain't nothin', we finally did it," Kaeem said.

"Yeah, I can't believe it. We goin' crush the dinner dance. I can't wait, how much you got Ka'?" he asked.

"I got a nickel," he responded.

"You cool then," said Malley.

"What's up with the chicks?" Kaeem asked.

"Ka' I ain't thinkin' 'bout them broads. I'm 'bout my chips right now," he stated.

"Yeah, I can dig it," responded Kaeem.

They wanted to go to the dinner dance right so they stopped by Connie's to grab a couple bags of weed to smoke. Rod had let Malley hold the Benz. He wanted him to go in style because he never had an opportunity as a kid to experience a graduation on that type of level. Fifty-Fourth Street was packed as ever. Patrons and limousines barricaded the streets. It sort of resembled a concert let out. As Malley and Kaeem got closer to the Wynne-Plaza, he started to lean in the seat and turned up "Set It Off" by Big Daddy Kane. Kaeem followed suit and leaned back. The loud bass from the system had the trunk pounding and windows rattling as they drove by. Heads immediately turned and mouths dropped as Malley and Kaeem was seen in that all white flying saucer. They stole the show and that was all there was to say. Simone and Turquoise definitely saw him, even though they were both on different sides of the street. Their eyes followed him until his brake lights could no longer be seen.

"Ka' and Malley doin' their thing. You better put a leash on him," spoke Shanda, trying to remind Turquoise what she was working with.

"Shanda he do what he want. He ain't my man," Turquoise replied.

"Stop frontin' like you don't dig him," she said.

"He alright, but he ain't my man," stated Turquoise trying to downplay the fact that she was feeling Malley.

"Ooh! There go that bitch Turquoise. I can't stand her," Simone said, being vindictive, speaking to Holly. She was really upset because Turquoise was seen with Malley. Although she was mad at him, she still showed some sort of interest by not backing down and continuing to compete.

Malley and Kaeem had came through like the president. They had tore the dinner dance up without even getting out. The way they crushed it was the talk of the night and probably would be the gossip for the next few months.

PART 2

NOW OR NEVER

CHAPTER 22

The next day Rod called a meeting. Malley was sort of caught off guard being he was still getting used to how the drug lane worked. On top of that, how he played his part going through the dinner dance was still on his mind, but he wasted no time with meeting up with his old head. As usual Rod awaited him at the chill spot. As Malley pulled up, Rod stood on the porch smoking a Newport. The fire from his cigarette got brighter as he took one last drag before tossing it and heading into the house. By this time Malley was out of the car and on his way behind him. Rod flopped on the couch and pulled his hoodie over his head. Malley didn't know what to make of it as he closed the door behind him.

"What's up ol' head?" Malley asked, a bit baffled. Rod looked him dead in the eyes with a look on his face that Malley had never seen before. Malley's mind was racing a mile a minute. After a brief pause he spoke.

"It's time," he stated.

"It's time for what?" Malley questioned uneasy. Out of nowhere Rod flipped his hoodie off taking another brief pause.

"It's time we take that trip I promised you," Rod stated.

"That's what's up," Malley replied, now feeling a sign of relief.

"But like I said before, when you reach your quota get out. Most muh'fucka's ain't lettin' you get out, let alone give you a choice. Remember your purpose because greed will put you in this shit deep," Rod explained. He had already let his mother know that he was taking him on the trip as a graduation present. Rod had already had their flight booked for Hawaii. The only thing left was to get Malley a passport. This trip was also an appreciation of his loyalty and how good he was at bringing back straight money. He explained to him how that was the core of his character. It all boiled down to being a good dude, because good dudes always got the best connects and high caliber women. On the flip side, good dudes would breed envy in turn which brought out the snakes. Watching dudes movements around money and women gave him an insight that most youngin's at his age wasn't aware of. He kept quiet as Rod was teaching him the game. That was the only way he would be able to soak it all up. He gave it to him raw and uncut. He knew deep down inside that he could be somebody if he stayed focused.

An unfamiliar voice spoke Rod's name as she made her way down the stairs. She immediately snatched Malley's attention as he never seen her before.

"Hey baby," Rod replied as she approached him, planting her lips on top of his.

"Hey cuttie," she said to Malley.

"Hi you doin'," he responded.

"Fine," she replied back, looking sexy.

"Yeah, Mal this is Zakeena, good peoples," he explained.

"I see, I see," he spoke, insinuating a compliment.

"You ready?" she questioned Rod.

"Yeah, I gotta go get his passport first," Rod said as they left and got in the rental car.

During the ride to the airport Malley was stuck on how bad Zakeena was. She was definitely top of the line, but all in all, it was in accordance to Rod's taste of women. As they pulled into the Philadelphia International, people were boarding and un-boarding their flights. Planes were also landing and taking off. Rod leaned over and kissed Zakeena before getting out. Him and his youngin' headed towards Gate 7 so they could board their flight. A slim chocolate flight stewardess escorted them to their seats. Rod let Malley have the window seat so he could enjoy the view. He knew that seeing planes fly by each other and disappearing into the clouds would blow his mind, being this was his first time flying. The fasten seat belt sign came on followed by the captain's instructions. Once each passenger fastened their seat belts, the plane began to move. Malley's stomach started to feel upset as the plane began to tilt back, taking off into the air. He didn't want to let Rod see him sweat, but when his ears started to pop he made an inquiry to Rod. Rod cracked a smile and gave him a pair of earplugs. As the plane continued to climb, the objects and people on the ground began to look as small as ants. Soaring smoothly through the air, all of a sudden, the plane moved unruly, experiencing turbulence. Malley's eyes enlarged, quickly grabbing both arms of his chair. Rod immediately convinced him that it was a normal part of a flight. Malley bought into his word, then relaxed. Rod then did his norm, prepping himself for some sleep only to try and cut most of the long flight to Hawaii down. Malley couldn't believe it, just like a kid trying to stay up all night for the first time, he tried it with the flight. Unable to fight his tiredness by the time his eyes opened again Rod was waking him up as the plane was preparing to land. The beautiful sight of Hawaii gave a description of nothing less than paradise. Each passenger embraced the semi-landing as the landing gear would screech each time it made contact with the runway, until all the wheels were planted equally.

"You ready youngin'?" Rod questioned.

"Yeah, I can't wait. This is beyond my imagination," Malley responded.

"You ain't seen nothin' yet," stated Rod as they waited in line to exit the plane. The expression invading Malley's face was indescribable. Beautiful Hawaiian women were everywhere giving all the visitors a warm welcome.

"Them chicks bad ass shit," spoke Malley.

"This is what it's about, the good life," Rod instilled.

"Enjoyin' yourself, huh?" inquired Malley.

"Yeah, you better believe it . . . Come on, let's see if this taxi will take us to our hotel," Rod said, approaching the cabdriver.

"May I help you?" the cabdriver asked.

"Yeah, do you know where the Madison Hotel is?" asked Rod.

"Sure, get in," the cabby stated, as Malley and Rod entered. The hotel was only a half an hour away from the airport. They arrived there in no time. The front of the hotel was immaculate with a marble floor entrance. The back of it had balconies attached to each room with a secluded swimming area. Rod paid the cabby, then headed towards the reception desk to check in. They both were tired from jetlag, but Rod needed to pick up some clothes for them for the night festivities. He was used to fighting through jetlag. This was something new to Malley. He was beat. It was all too much for him to take in, so he let him catch up on some rest.

CHAPTER 23

Rod had been gone almost all that day grabbing the hottest lay for them and Malley was still sleeping like a baby when he got back. He tapped him repeatedly until he woke up.

"What's up?" Malley questioned, as he stretched in a tiresome tone.

"Get up, man I've been gone all day," Rod emphasized.

"I'm up, I just ordered two Hawaiian Stromboli's," spoke Malley.

"What you know about Hawaiian Stromboli's?" Rod asked, knowing he never been out there before.

"Them jawns be sayin' somethin' with a Maiti. I grabbed us a few Sergiotech and T.I. sweat suits. We throw them on with the all white hoe catchers. Trust me the chicks is gonna be all over us tonight at the club," said Rod.

"Well, I'ma take a shower so I can throw it on and we can be out," Malley stated. Rod smirked, then shook his head. He was admiring his little cousin's style.

The night came and the music from Club Wi' pounded out of the speakers as they made their way onto the scene. Rod had peeled off two crispy c-notes to the bouncers to look pass Malley. They let him in with no problem. The baddest women Malley ever saw was right before his eyes. The hood couldn't produce those types of women if it wanted to. They were a whole different class of exotic phenom's. Two beautiful women were dancing erotically by the bar, sipping on their drinks with their eyes locked on Malley and Rod.

"What's up, which one you want?" Rod asked.

"The tall one with the long hair and fat ass," he responded.

"Ay sexy come here for a minute, somebody wanna meet you," Rod said, as he flagged over to their direction. She made her way over there with no problem.

"Hi," she spoke.

"Hey . . .," Rod said aloud, then put his arm around her, whispering in her ear as he slipped her $200. She smoothly stuffed the two crispy bills between her cleavage, grabbing Malley by his hand, once Rod took his arm from around her. She led him towards the bathroom. Rod gave Malley a wink as she slowly pulled him away.

She took lead with confidence straight into the ladies room. As it was semi-packed they found their way to the last empty stall. She pushed him in it, closing it behind her. Malley felt like an animal trapped by its predator. This was totally different from sleeping with the younger chicks back home. This was an aggressive woman who was about to seriously show him the ropes. Malley was kind of nervous, but avoided to show her. She wasted no time, leaning closer, sticking her tongue in his ear, grabbing his manhood. As she continued to massage him, he felt himself beginning to grow in his pants. This is what she was waiting for. His heart started to race, feeling the intensity run through his body. She dropped to her knees, pulling out his stiff sword. She licked the side of his shaft, causing him to sigh, then making her way to the tip of the head, making circles around it, which drove him crazy.

"All shit," Malley sighed, looked at the ceiling then back at her. She looked up at him noticing his enjoyment, then began to move her mouth back and forth over top of him. His breathing became heavier while she was giving him the time of his life. He found his palm on the top of her head moving with each of her bobs. He could feel himself ready to explode from her nonstop performance. Malley had never gotten his dick sucked so good. Unable to hold back his orgasm, he released into her mouth. Unfazed by his release she sucked harder, draining what was left, while he found himself grabbing onto the bathroom wall trying to stand. She literally almost dropped him to his knees. The mystery woman rose to her feet licking her lips. She blew Malley a kiss before exiting. It was like he had an outer body experience. He wiped himself off, then pulled his pants up. He took a deep breath, making his way back to the bar where Rod was seated.

"Oh, there you go. I was gettin' worried," Rod said, being sarcastic.

"Yo . . . man, she was good," stated Malley, still on cloud nine. Rod laughed reminiscing on how he felt when he had gotten his first dick suck in Hawaii.

"Hunn," Rod said passing him a joint of Hawaiian Gold. This weed was exotic and hard to find in the states. For the most part it was actually gold. Malley took a pull, trying to hold it in like regular weed. For a quick few seconds he was able, until the smoke forced its way out of his mouth followed by his coughs. His eyes instantly watered. Again Rod laughed at his younger cousin trying to hang with a big dawg. He took the joint back from him and inhaled.

"Damn, that's some killa," spoke Malley.

"So what's it gonna be? You can chill now and stop," stated Rod.

"I don't know yet. I'm thinkin' about it," he responded uncertain.

"This shit don't last forever. You know I ain't gonna tell you nothin' wrong," Rod said.

"Yeah, I know," replied Malley. They finished having a good time that night, which was the last thing Malley remembered after waking up back at the hotel. The smell of cheese eggs, pancakes and sausage filled the air. Rod had Malley's plate ready. All he had to do was dive in.

"Good lookin'," spoke Malley, half asleep and hungry as a hostage.

"We got a beautiful day ahead of us," Rod expressed. They ended up at one of Hawaii's finest beaches. It wasn't nothing but gorgeous women walking throughout the sand in skimpy bikinis. Rod and Malley did a lot that day. It was the first time Malley had gotten a chance to ride on a jet ski. After constantly falling into the water, he got the hang of it in no time. Two Hawaiian girls removed their tops as they sat in their speedboat, watching Malley and Rod race by. For the next several hours they had fun. As they headed back, the horizon of Hawaii's skyline was setting. Capturing this scene was something that Malley had only seen on a commercial or in a magazine. The more and more that was revealed to him, the larger his love grew for the game. This was a world hidden to a few, but known to many. This graduation present was a gift and a curse. It literally was setting a foundation to keep him glued on the highway of the game, regardless of wanting to take a back seat. Also the fact that him seeing how a thing so ugly could birth a thing so beautiful, didn't help at all. When they got back to the hotel they just decided to call it a night and lounge.

"Mal, what's up with your chicks? You fix that situation?" he asked inquiring.

"Naw, not yet. I'm kind of caught up right now, but I'ma work on it. The crazy thing about it all is that I dig the both of them," he replied.

"I feel you, but pay attention to the one who don't ask you for nothin'. Trust me, that's the one who dig you for you," stated Rod.

"Got you," said Malley.

"We got a lot to count when we get back. I got somethin' big lined up. Get some sleep. We out of here tomorrow," Rod spoke, then headed to his room.

CHAPTER 24

Their flight departed at six in the morning. Surprisingly the airport or plane weren't too crowded. Rod ended up sleeping during most of the flight as Malley slept off and on, thinking about everything he had just experienced, but the fact was that he couldn't get Simone or Turquoise off of his mind. Only in a semi-trance, Malley opened his eyes to the sound of the flight attendant's voice. She informed him that they were preparing to land. Malley woke Rod up so he could get ready. Rod stretched and yawned at the same time.

What we 'bout to land?" he inquired.

"She said in about five minutes," Malley replied.

Rod got himself together as the plane began to land. Malley felt a different level of confidence now that he had seen another part of the world. Just that trip alone showed him that it was bigger than Philly. By the time they landed, a different chick was waiting to pick them up. Malley got in the back, then she pulled off. Kareema took Cobbs Creek Parkway all the way down 63rd Street, until she got to 63rd & Chestnut. Malley had his car parked behind the Amoco Gas Station in a drive alley. This was his little incognito spot. After he

113

got out and thanked Rod for everything, he got in his car and drove home.

The smell of home cooked food smacked him in the face as he opened the door. The food from Hawaii was good and unique, but it wasn't nothing like a home cooked meal. His mom turned around with a huge Kool-Aid smile on her face, happy to see her son. He walked over to her and gave her a huge hug and kiss.

"Mommy missed you," she spoke excited.

"I missed you too," replied Malley.

"How was your trip?" she asked.

"I can't even begin mom, it was . . . it was fun," he responded, a little hesitant.

"Well, I'm glad you had a good time. Dinner is ready, so get yourself together and get ready to eat," his mom told him.

"Alright," Malley said, tired, making his way to the couch. Not even a minute after he took his sneakers off, he passed out. His mom returned with his plate only to see her son out of it. She shook her head with a smile, then put his dinner in the microwave. Later that night he ended up finding his plate, eating some of momma's home cooking, then he ended up passing out again.

The next morning Malley was awakened by the pounding sound of a fist banging on his door. BOOM . . . BOOM . . . BOOM . . . BOOM . . . BOOM . . . BOOM . . . BOOM . . . BOOM . . . BOOM . . . BOOM!

"Jamal, open this goddamn door!" his mom said, sounding furious.

"Alright, alright," he responded, wondering why she was banging on his door like the police. BOOM . . .

BOOM . . . BOOM! She continued to bang on his door until he opened it, busting her way into his room.

"Where is it?!" she asked.

"Where is what?" he questioned.

"Boy don't play with me. If you got any drugs in my house you better get it out of here," she stated, fuming.

"What are you talkin' about?" Malley asked again, trying to put two and two together.

"Boy! It's all over the news. Rodney just got busted!" she explained to him.

"What?!" Malley asked, shocked as a knot grew in his throat.

"Yeah, they say he sold ten kilos to a Federal agent!" his mom shouted angrily.

"Mom, you can't believe the news," he responded, trying to fool himself of the unfortunate news.

"Boy! I know my nephew. Don't play with my intelligence!" she stated, not buying into Malley's game.

"Mom, calm down. It ain't nothin' in here," he explained to her, hoping she simmered down. A thousand and one things were going through his mind. He knew his mom was heated, her eyes said it all. He had no choice but to continue to take the ear lashing and most and foremost hope for the best.

"Ain't no calm down! You holdin' for him? I better not find out, you're out in them streets hustlin' for him," she spoke in anger.

"Damn! This the shit R' was talkin' 'bout, now what?" Malley questioned himself as he went into a zone. Rod getting locked up threw a monkey wrench in his routine. He knew that the Feds had probably tapped all their family phones. It was like being stuck in cement. All he could do was try and wait for Rod to call and reach out to somebody in the family or have one of his chicks get a message to him. Playing into the waiting game was frustrating, so he called Simone.

"Hello?" an unfamiliar voice questioned.

"Can I speak to Simone?" Malley asked.

"Who's callin'?" she inquired.

"Malley," he answered.

"She's not here," she replied.

"Alright, can you tell her I called?" he stated, ready to hang up.

"Oh, hold on, she just walked in," she replied, handing Simone the phone.

"Hello?" said Simone.

"What's up?" Malley asked.

"Who this?" she questioned.

'Malley," he responded.

"Oh, so you finally decided to call me, huh?" Simone stated, showing some concern that she missed him.

"It ain't like that," said Malley.

"Well, what's it like then?" she asked.

"I been was gonna call you, but I just got back in the city," Malley explained.

"Boy, don't you know ya cousin, Ro . . .," she said, unable to finish her statement.

"Yeah, yeah, I know," Malley said, quickly cutting her off. He wasn't sure if them boys was listening to their conversations.

"Dag, why you cut me off?" she asked, not really understanding the intricate's of the game.

"Look, we can't rap right now, but I need to see you," he expressed.

"You need to see that dirt bomb," she stated, talking about Turquoise.

"Come on S' not now, shit real serious," he emphasized.

"So what you goin' come get me?" she asked.

"I can't, I'm layin' low right now. Call a cab. I'ma pay him when you get here," Malley replied.

"Alright," she answered.

CHAPTER 25

Even though it was his older cousin who got knocked off, he was still paranoid as if the Feds knew about him. No one knew how long they were watching Rod before they came to indict him. Which meant that they were on to most of his moves and the players he dealt with, Malley being one of his up and coming youngin's.

Malley peeped out of the blinds when he heard a car horn beep. As he expected it was Simone getting out of the cab. He gave the cabdriver thirty dollars to cover the tab. Immediately he returned back into the house.

"What's this about? Ya mom here?" Simone questioned curiously.

"Naw, we cool. I'm stressin' like shit. You know the situation with my peoples," Malley implied, speaking about Rod.

"Yeah, he'll probably be alright," she responded.

"I gotta like chill for a minute, at least until I know what's goin' on," he said.

"Listen Malley, I like you a lot, but you can't be tryna play me. You know how many bols chasin' me?" she said, posing a rhetorical question.

"I'm sayin' that's neither here nor there. You gonna throw that in my face?" he questioned as she put the fact out there.

"You gotta choose me or that winch. The decision is up to you," Simon stated sternly.

"I know. I got a lot on my mind. My cousin really dig you. He said you the one," Malley explained to her. He believed in his heart that she was good for him, but he just didn't have no plans on letting Turquoise go at the moment.

"You want somethin' to drink or anythin'?" he asked.

"Yeah, you can get me a soda," she replied.

Malley returned with her soda, then they departed to his bedroom. He wasted no time turning on 12 Play by R-Kelly. He couldn't go wrong with some R' playing. The girls were crazy over 12 Play. He let that bump as he laid back on his bed, admiring how beautiful Simone was. She took bashful sips of her soda watching how Malley looked at her.

"What?" she questioned.

"Nothin'. It's just you're beautiful, you bad," he told her.

"I know you say that to all your little girlfriends," Simone stated.

"Not at all, Simone. I'm feelin' you," he said, as he made his way over to her. He sat right beside her, running the back of his hand down the side of her face. The warmth of his hand sent chills down her spine. Her eyes begin to lower. In turn, he stared into them with his bedroom eyes. He had never been with Simone sexually but if he was going to try to get some, now was the time. He increased his moves by placing his hand on her thigh, slowly rubbing it up and down. Simone just sat there quietly falling into his seduction. Malley could see that his actions were taking a toll on her, her nipples was piercing her shirt.

"Stop," she said in a low voice, really wanting him to continue.

"I want you baby," said Malley, whispering into her ear. That's not all he did. He also blew his warm breath into it, invading it with his tongue. She began to hiss and pant.

He slowly started to undress her, exposing her sexy matching bra and panties. He laid her down gentle and peeled them off. The sight of her smooth skin and V-shaped peach increased his blood flow. Malley couldn't fight back the urge of how she was making him feel inside his pants. He was beyond turned on and he wanted to get in between her legs badly. His kisses worked their way up from the top of her feet, to the most sacred part on her body. As he looked up at Simone, her mixture of pleasure and innocence was written all across her face. Malley rose up, next wanting to be inside her and Simone was ready as well.

"You got any condoms?" she questioned.

"Naw, but I can get one," he replied.

"I want to do it with you Malley, just don't cum in me," she said, clinching his chest with her fingernails. Her main concern was not getting pregnant, but the way he was making her feel she was willing to take a chance. Malley wasted no time at his opportunity to be with Simone. He took his time, entering her slowly. She tensed up a bit as he continued to go all the way in. As he moved in and out finding his rhythm, she gave into a feeling of pleasure and pain. The more he stroked her, hitting her spot, the more she buried her nails into his back. He knew that she was enjoying how he was tearing her up, so he stroked even faster.

"Oh, Malley, you feel so good," Simone expressed, taking all of him.

"That's right take it," he replied, feeling himself.

"Oh . . .," said Simone as she felt every inch of Malley's manhood. He gripped the top of his headboard, pinning her down to where she couldn't move. With each thrust he made, his headboard knock against the wall, something he always wanted to do. Each time he heard the clacking of the headboard grow louder, the faster and harder he pumped her in and out. With the bed now rocking and squeaking, Simone found herself trying to squirm her way from out of his grasp. Malley was chasing his orgasm, but at the same time was sexing Simone out of her mind. She had never experienced this type of performance before. This was the wettest she had ever been, feeling all of him in her stomach Simone continued to fight Malley as he continued to put his work in.

"Damn you feel good," Malley said, keeping up the pace, not knowing how long he would be able to hold himself back from exploding.

"Ssss . . . Oh God, Oh God . . . shit!" Simone cried as her body shook out of control, releasing a waterfall of warm fluids. She just reached her first orgasm unbeknownst to her. Not knowing what just happened, she got scared for a brief second, then realized that she may just have had an orgasm. Simone's moisture and tightness drove Malley into overdrive. She felt so good to him, before he knew it, he found himself ejaculating in her, breaking the same rule that he promised to abide by. After his body stopped contorting, he laid body to body with her. Once she landed back on earth and regained her normal state of mind, it dawned on her that he had came inside of her.

"Boy, you came in me. I told you to pull out," she said, snatching the covers off of him.

"I tried, that shit was good. I ain't mean it," Malley said, laying there totally spun.

"Boy, I better not get pregnant. We wasn't supposed to be doin' it anyway. You already got a girl. How could I've been so dumb," Simone stated with regrets.

"Why you trippin'?" he asked quickly as things seemed like déjà vu.

"I just don't wanna get hurt," she responded.

"Baby girl I ain't gonna hurt you," replied Malley.

"That's what your mouth say," she stated, not buying it one bit.

"I got you S', I'm feeling' you," he spoke quickly on his toes.

"I'm just so scarred to trust you," Simone said, letting him know her deepest fear.

"I ain't gonna betray you," he replied.

"I hope not," she stated, concerned.

"I'ma be chillin' so, I'ma need you to get with Ka' and J' and find out what Rod bail is. If anybody other than them ask, you didn't see or hear from me," Malley instilled, panicking not knowing what to expect. Rod always taught him that security was first.

"Alright," she responded. They both got themselves together. Simone took a shower and got dressed. Her taxi arrived in no time. Malley gave her a quick kiss before she got into the cab. This was all perfect timing as his mom would be home any minute. He continued putting a few dollars away in his safe.

CHAPTER 26

The following day Simone kept her word and went down 62nd Street to take care of what Malley asked her to do. Ka' stood in front of Pat's, accompanied with a few of his friends. This was the Chinese store where a lot of the youngin's hustled at.

"Hey Kaeem?" spoke Simone as she walked up to him.

"What's up Simone? What you doin' down these parts?" Kaeem inquired.

"Malley told me to get with you, he's stressin'. He said to ask you or J' did Rodney get a bail and he ain't usin' no phone, for y'all to just come through," Simone explained.

"Tell him Rod fell on a sixty count indictment. Plus, the ten they caught him with. Shit lookin' ugly right now. He still down the Federal buildin' down 6th & Market. Just tell him to lay low and that the Feds is all in the hood. We'll see him tomorrow," he replied.

"Alright," she said, then left. Simone showed her loyalty by keeping her word.

After she brought him up to speed as to what was Rod's status, he commended her and felt somewhat relieved that he knew what was going on. Deep down inside he was hurting that his old head was knocked off. Although this was his way out, he felt as though he owed it to Rod to be in his corner a hundred percent. He knew it would be a roll of the dice if he kept hustling since he wasn't sure if the Feds were aware of him. He figured being he wasn't the big man on the totem-pole, he might be on the safe side to make a few moves here and there. Later that night Kaeem ended up meeting with him.

"What's up Mal?" Ka' asked.

"Man . . . I've been on some other shit since R' got knocked. My mind just ain't been right," Malley told him, kind of depressed.

"He holdin' up strong, he got the toughest lawyers in the city. He said to tell you he sends his luv, that this is part of the game and that he want you to come up next week with us," Kaeem explained.

"Without doubt, I'ma be there. Ka' I'm 'bout to rip it," Malley said with the intentions on rising in the game.

"Mal, you trippin'?" Kaeem responded, not understanding his logic.

"Ka' it's to the top," he replied as if he already made up his mind.

"Yeah, alright. I'm with you. I just hope you know what you doin'. I see you and Simone vibin' now," said Kaeem.

"Yeah, that's my boo. We got feelin's for each other," he said, with a smile on his face.

"What's up with what's her name?" he asked.

"Who Turquoise?" he questioned.

"Yeah, what's up with her?" Kaeem inquired.

"She ain't called me and I ain't called her either. I ain't seen her since the graduation," spoke Malley.

"Yo, I gotta breeze," Ka' said as he had a lot of things to do as well. He just wanted to let him know the latest with Rod.

"Alright, send my luv," he stated.

"No doubt," Ka' responded, shaking his hand and giving him a hug.

Despite Malley's appetite for the game, he knew he had to lay low until the heat died down. Simone began to show him that she was all for him by spending as much time with him as she could. They definitely started to get closer to each other.

CHAPTER 27

The following week came and it was time to see Rod. Malley had stayed over his Aunt Rita's house so they could all leave from there in the morning. He spoke to his Aunt Rita as she came downstairs. She told Kaeem to make sure the stove was off before they left. Lil J' had to go over his great grandmother's house to pull up weeds, so he missed the trip. Malley's Aunt Rita was thorough. She understood the in's and out's of the game, but wouldn't allow her sons to get involved in it at no cost. They left early so they could beat traffic. It was difficult to get a parking spot downtown at a certain time. His Aunt Rita ended up finding a parking spot on a side street. As they got out of the car and approached the Federal building a ton of mixed emotions hit Malley. U.S. Marshalls and undercover agents were everywhere. Once they entered the building a heavyset corrections officer awaited them at the reception desk.

"Excuse me, we're here to see Rodney Robinson," Ms. Rita stated to the officer.

"What is his F.B.I. number?" asked the C.O.

"78978-066," Ms. Rita told him.

"Okay, I am calling his block," the C.O. replied.

After going through the metal detectors and scanners to get checked, it took about fifteen minutes before they were allowed to enter the visiting room. This day it was pretty crowded. Visitors were entering and leaving and Kaeem and Malley were checking all the women out.

"Okay, ma'am your visit is waiting. You can go right through that door," the C.O. told Ms. Rita, pointing to the visitor's room.

They each walked through the steel door that other visitors walked in and out of. The door made a funny cranking sound as it slowly opened. Malley grew impatient as it seemed the door was taking forever to remove the barrier between him and his old head. As it finally came to a stop, Rod stood on the other side dressed in his tans. Appreciation covered his face at the sight of seeing his family. He greeted his Aunt Rita with a hug and kiss on the cheek. She embraced him back, showing unconditional love.

"What's up Ka'?" Rod asked, paying homage to his little cousin.

"Ain't nothin'. What's up with you?" Kaeem questioned.

"I'm good. What's up Mal?" he asked, then escorted them to the seating area. Rod was happy to see his family but seeing his number one youngin' made his day.

"You ol'head," he stated instantly.

"Yeah, I can dig it," Rod mentioned, just enjoying the moment.

"Me and Kaeem are going to let you two catch up on things," his Aunt Rita stated, creating some space between the two. She was aware that Rod was giving Malley packages here and there, but she just played it off.

"Alright, what's up lil buddie?" he asked.

"Man . . . ever since they grabbed you, I've been layin' low, playin' it by ear," he stated.

"Yeah, as soon as I got back you know I had that thing in motion," he explained.

"Yeah, yeah I remember," Malley agreed.

"Man . . . the nigga was the Feds the whole time. They gave him cars and cribs. I mean he knew slang and all. I also fell on lil screw and 'em indictment from down North," Rod said, breaking the bad news to him.

"What's up with your bail?" Malley inquired.

"I got a ransom, that shit a mil-plus," he spoke.

"Damn!" he blurted out in anger, trying to think of a way out.

"I got two lawyers. They tough as nails. They want sixty a piece," said Rod.

"You covered?" Malley asked, needing to know how he could be of some assistance.

"I got that, but they seized most of my wheels. I still got a nice piece of change tucked and the salon's is cool," Rod informed him.

"R', I luv you too death. Anythin', I mean anythin', that gotta be handled, let me know and it's done, no rap!" Malley said, fuming hearing this disturbing news. He couldn't fathom the fact that his old head's run may have came to an end.

"Cool out, I need you to stay focused in school and look after ya mom. You goin' to Brook next year, right?" he asked.

"Yeah."

"You know that's a fashion school right?"

"Yeah, I know."

"Look, like I was tellin' you. This the flip side to the good side. You gotta take the bitter with the sweet," Rod informed.

"I'm on point, ol' head," spoke Malley.

"If you gonna play this game, play with your eyes open. Watch everybody and stay low. I got somethin' nice for you when the time is right. One of my chicks gonna get in contact with you and pass off," Rod said, possibly getting ready to pass the torch.

"What you want back?" Malley inquired immediately.

"They'll give you a number, just get paid."

"I got you."

"Oh yeah, keep some tint on ya wheel, tune it down a lil and keep you a few burna's," said Rod, wanting Malley to have some guns in his arsenal to protect himself.

"How we gonna communicate?"

"Through Ka', that phone thing is dead."

"I feel that," stated Malley.

"Look, let me yell at auntie for a few."

"Alright," Malley replied, giving his big cousin a handshake and hug.

CHAPTER 28

Malley went over to the vending machines, letting Ka' and his Aunt Rita talk with Rod for some time. He felt good being able to speak with him. Sort of like releasing the weight of the world from off his shoulders. This day Malley had made his decision to forge ahead in the game, disregarding his way out. The fact of his old head getting ready to fight for his life played a part in trying to be there for him. In his mind he was in debt to him. A debt that he wanted to make sure he squared away. After he got home he did exactly what Rod told him to do. He went to try to buy some heat. He knew the perfect person to point him in the right direction. If he didn't have it, nobody had it. Malley headed right to Larry Gunther's. As he pulled in front of his house, Larry stood on his porch talking with a few other smokers, trying to score. He hit the horn, then rolled down his tinted window. Once Larry recognized who it was, Malley then signaled for him to come over to the car.

"What's up son?" spoke Larry Gunther as he called everybody in the hood son.

"I need a burna, you got one?" Malley said with a serious look on his face, watching through his rearview mirror. Larry looked both ways before answering.

"Yeah, yeah, I got somethin' for you," stated Larry.

"Alright, grab it for me and take this ride with me," he told Larry.

"Shit, I ain't gotta grab it, it's on me," said Larry, getting ready to lift up his shirt.

"Yo, yo, yo, you trippin', just get it," spoke Malley. Larry didn't care if the cops was turning the corner. He was trying to get his next fix. Malley pulled off, driving around the corner to Arch Street, where the drive alley led to the top of Race Street. Larry pulled out a black .380, looking fairly new with a few scratches on it.

"Pops this shit better work," Malley said.

"I ain't gonna sell you no broke shit," Larry said. He had a lot of game with him, so Malley wanted to make sure it worked and if it did it would do for now. Seven shots was good enough for him. That would back anybody away if they were cornered. Larry put it in his hand. Malley turned it from side to side, examining it. He didn't have any experience in shooting guns, but it was only one way to find out to see if it worked. They both got out of the car. Malley walked back towards the trailer in the drive alley, pointed it in the air and squeezed. POP . . . POP. . . POP . . .POP! The gun sounded, causing his ears to ring a little but a feeling unlike no other ran through his body. He quickly tucked the gun and got back into the car. It was broad daylight so he didn't need no nosy neighbors looking out their windows.

"See, I told you it work," Larry said, getting back into the car, waiting for his fix.

"Yeah, yeah I want this joint, how much?" he asked.

"Give me ten rocks."

"Got you. You got some more bullets?"

"No, but my boy does."

"Alright," Malley said, pulling off. This was the first gun he ever bought. Not really wanting any trouble with the streets, he just listened to what Rod told him about protecting himself.

Later that night he called Simone. He needed to check up on his baby girl. Surprisingly she was asleep, so he decided to give Turquoise a ring.

"Hello? Can I speak to Turquoise?" he asked.

"Who this?" she questioned.

"Malley."

"Hey stranger, what you only call when you want some?" Turquoise asked, being smart.

"Naw, cool out, I've been goin' through some serious shit lately," he expressed.

"And how old are you? Talkin' 'bout goin' through some serious shit. So I guess that's why you ain't been to school either?" she questioned.

"Somethin' like that, but what's been up with you?" he questioned.

"You know, doin' what I do," she stated.

"What's that?" asked Malley.

"Keepin' you dudes chasin' and them bitches jealous," she said, being her usual cocky self.

"I can dig it," Malley said, unsurprised.

"Where your lil girlfriend at?" she sarcastically asked.

"Come on Turquoise, cut that short. I called to buss it with you, not about nobody else. You doin' ya thing. I'm doin' mines," he explained plainly and to the point.

"Alright, Mr. sensitive, when you comin' back through?" Turquoise asked.

"I don't know, why what's up?"

"You know you put ya thing down. I need some more of that," she emphasized.

"It's gonna be a part two," he emphasized.

"Ooh . . . I'm scared," Turquoise replied sarcastically.

"I don't want you to be scared, be ready."

"I was born ready."

"I'ma tear you out the frame," he said, falling into back to back trash talk.

"Yeah, yeah, yeah, we'll see," she replied.

"Alright you won. I'ma hit you later. I gotta take care of somethin'."

"Ain't no alright, you better call boy."

"Got you."

Turquoise had her claws deep into him. The attraction between the two was unbearable. Even after a few times of trying to resist her, he somehow always found himself embracing the urge to forfeit it. Whether he knew it or not, Malley was trapped in a love triangle between himself, Turquoise and Simone.

CHAPTER 29

The morning had came, school was out and the pools were open. Malley had made his way down 62nd Street to see if the young bols he supplied earlier with samples had the block back jumping. He was switching up his cars from rentals to squatters. This was not only throwing the hood off, but the law as well, if they were on to him. Lil J' and a couple of neighborhood dudes posted up in front of Pat's and Jo'Jo's. 6151 was even crowded. The dude had fiends coming from all over scouring for crack. The hood was now getting back into rhythm from the heat Rod brought to it from him getting indicted. Malley's tinted up Cavalier had Lil J' and about two other soldiers out there on alert as his slow creep came to a stop.

"Yo, who that?" Lil J' questioned in a stern tone, trying to pinpoint who was in the car. Without a sign of acknowledgment, Lil J' reached underneath his shirt gesturing like he had a gun. Malley sat behind the tint laughing to himself, while he watched his cousin act like he was really holding it down. He shook his head as J' continued to mouth words. Enough was enough. He rolled the window down so J' could be at ease.

"Yo man, chill, it's me," spoke Malley as J' vied to get a closer look.

"Bol, you crazy ridin' around with ya windows smoked out," said J', approaching the passenger side.

"This how I'm doin' it," he replied.

"Bol, you almost got somethin'," said Lil J'.

"J' you ain't hurtin' nothing, seein' nothin' get hurt," he said.

"Where Ka' at?"

"He shot to Maroney's to grab a water ice," J' replied.

"Come on, hop in. Lets spin around there real quick," Malley insisted.

By the time they got around the corner Kaeem was standing in line and 63rd Street took its normal form of being crowded, anytime Maroney's would open. Everybody and their mother were waiting in line for their famous water ice's and cheese pretzels. Sundaes and Gelato's was also Maroney's signature products. You could see that the ambiance of summer was present. Cars were driving by with knocking systems playing "Summertime" by the Fresh Prince and the sound of loud pipes roaring through the air from motorcycles being wheeled had set the tone for the summertime antics, never mind all of the girls wearing their daisy dukes or coochie cutters with their toes out. These elements altogether spoke its own language.

"There go Ka' right there," said Malley, taping the horn, pulling alongside of Maroney's. Kaeem quickly turned around trying to make out who was sitting behind the tint. Malley cracked the window a little to where Kaeem could only see his eyes and the top of his fitted hat.

"Yo Ka'?" Lil J' spoke calling him in a deep voice. Still fighting to see who was in the car, he began to move closer as the muffled voice started to ring a bell. Malley ended the charade, rolling the window all the way down.

"Man . . . y'all trippin'. I see you and J' got jokes, huh?" he asked.

"Man soldier up. What's up though?" Malley inquired.

"Ain't nothing," said Ka'.

"I got a taste for a sundae. That's why I shot up here," Malley stated.

"Yeah right. I know J' told you I was up here," spoke Kaeem, not convinced.

"Sike naw, you on point. Maroney's is doin' it," said Malley.

"Yeah I know," spoke J'.

"Damn! Look at shorty, they out here today," spoke Malley with his eyes on a bad chick waiting in line.

"I know," Kaeem replied.

Malley changed his mind and ordered his usual tutti fruiti. As he paid for his water ice he pulled out his beeper, checking his latest pages. Now playing his part to the fullest. Anybody who knew Rod instantly would be able to notice how some of Rod's ways had rubbed off on him. He was surely growing into himself at a fast pace. Malley saw a few chicks watching him from his peripheral, so he put a bit more emphasis on the show he was putting on. The new found attention he was getting inspired his ambition to keep getting to a dollar. After they all ordered and kicked game to some of the females who waited in line, Malley pretty much patrolled the hood to make sure things were running back to normal. Kaeem rode shotgun while J' played the back seat.

"Ka' did R' get with you yet?" asked Malley.

"Yeah," he replied.

"What's up with him?"

"He got a court date for next month, but he maintainin'," said Kaeem.

"I can dig it."

"I see you got the duce crankin'," said Lil J'.

"J' I'm tryin' take it to the next level," Malley explained.

"You really got ya mind made up, huh?" questioned Kaeem.

"I gotta get my miz out the jets one day."

"I hear you," Ka' stated.

"What's up with the county fair?" asked J'.

"Why, where it's gonna be?" Malley questioned.

"On Girard Ave. Damn near the whole Fairmount Park goin' be lit up. We should shoot through tonight," J' insisted.

"Yeah we can shoot through, you with it Ka'?" Malley asked.

"It's whatever," Kaeem responded.

"Alright, we shootin' down there. I'ma get with y'all like, eight, eight-thirty," Malley told them.

He dropped Kaeem and Lil J' off, then went to check on the posts. After finding out that everything was cool, he drove up to Haddington Recreation Center. Haddington always had a basketball tournament going on at least twice a week. With nothing else to do and Rod's situation on his mind, this was his way of clearing it. An older cat named Braheem that he took a like into was one of the top ballers at Haddington's. Braheem and his crew was playing another high ranked team. This team was led by Ty-Ty. He had an all around game as well. When these two balled they would bring out the chicks so wherever the chicks were, the dudes followed.

Rod would make it his business to make sure the summer league tournaments for the summer ran, as he used this as an outlet to keep the youngin's out of trouble. From new equipment to paid referees, he gave back as much as he could. Security monitored the doors while the chicks filled the bleachers. Braheem finished stretching his legs making his way on the court. Winning the tap ball, Braheem drove right to the rim laying it up. The move he put on the other player sent the crowd in an uproar. Ty-Ty wasn't going to allow Braheem to take the show. He immediately went to work slamming on one of their players. They both put on a show back and forth, keeping the spectators jumping out of their seats. With only five seconds on the clock and down by two, Ty-Ty was playing tight defense on Braheem, making it difficult for him to make it across half court. Noticing that two seconds was only left, he pushed his way as close as he could to the three point line and rose up. With Ty-Ty's hand in his face he was still able to get the shot off. Everybody watched the ball release from his hands with the clock on zero, aiming for the basket. It soared through the air in slow motion. The anticipation of the ball going in or out couldn't come any faster. Finally, the ball went through, all net. Braheem and his team ran out of the gym like they won the championship. The spectators went crazy, even Malley felt somewhat carefree. This few hours of escape came right in handy for him. As time wound down, he went home before he got ready to meet up with Ka' and J'.

CHAPTER 30

Malley entered his house, heading straight to the refrigerator. He loved his mother's homemade Kool-Aid. He saw that she was occupied talking on the phone, so he did what every kid loved to do—drink from the jug. He quickly tried to tilt the jug to his mouth only to hear his mother telling him that he better not be drinking out of the container. Being she was too late, he hurried up and took another swig before answering.

"I ain't," he responded, wiping his mouth.

"And I was born yesterday. Get your ass out of my refrigerator," she said, knowing he was lying. He walked out of the kitchen like a little kid with a smile on his face. He approached his mom, trying to give her a kiss on the cheek.

"Boy stop, you see I'm on the phone," she replied, weaving away from him.

"How was your day?" he asked.

"Boy if you don't..." She paused, trying to find something to throw at him. He laughed then took off.

Malley loved his mother dearly. He went to his room and turned on some "Nice & Smooth." He chose to relax some until it was time to roll out. To be a

143

young buck he was starting to get some nice money. Actually, this was the first time he ever saw this level of life. After crashing and getting dressed, he double checked to see if his mom needed anything. She was okay. She just wanted him to be careful. Malley knew that she didn't approve of what he was doing, but he also saw how she wasn't constantly down his throat. He hopped in his car and headed over to Ka's.

Lil J' and Kaeem stood on Market Street as Malley came from the south side of 62nd. He hit the horn, getting their attention so he could pull over and pull off. It was eight-twenty so he was sort of on time. They got in then drove off.

"Okay Ka' I see you got that shit on," Malley said, giving him his props.

"Man . . . this ain't about nothin', you killin' 'em with that peach, Mal," Kaeem said flipping it right back on him.

"Man . . . that canary yellow killin' 'em. Plus, J' got that flamingo pink and white Lo shit on," Malley emphasized. They all wore Polo. Ralph Lauren had different variations of his brand but the Polo Chino collection was the most popular at the time.

They were rolling to the fair right. Malley wanted to have it all around the board and whoever rolled with him was going to have it the same way. In his mind he wasn't playing games no more. You didn't have to like him but you were going to respect him. By the time they got down the bottom, it was hot as fish grease. A major bol named Ray-Ray had just got killed. He was real crafty and being slimy would get you nowhere but put in the ground. Unmarked homicide cars staked out on every corner.

"It's hot as shit down here," J' stated, second guessing before he went into Pebbles and Bam-Bams.

"Yeah I know. Grab a dub and we out," Malley told J'. He was in and out like a robbery. They smoked two blunts before they got there, feeling it.

The sky had became dark and the bright yellow and white lights on the rides and concession stands lit up the fair. Fairmount Park got jam packed from the nonstop patrons arriving. The females were everywhere. It was impossible for Malley, Kaeem and J' to keep their eyes on every female crossing their path without choosing one in particular. It looked like a baby Greek picnic. These chicks were dressed to impress and their attire was skin tight, leaving nothing to the imagination. The toughest of the toughest were out. Malley found a parking spot and jumped out feeling himself. Well, they all did. They bought two hundred tickets a piece to keep them occupied.

"Here you go sweetheart, enjoy yourself," the ticket conductor said, flirting with Malley as she handed him his tickets. He picked right up on her coming on to him, so he pulled them out of her hand slowly.

"It's gonna be hard without your company," Malley said, following up his gesture.

"Oh is that right?" she questioned.

"Absolutely," Malley replied walking off.

"Okay playa," spoke Ka', noticing his confidence.

"You see how she was comin' at me?" Malley asked, elated.

"You doin' a lil somethin', somethin'," stated Ka'.

"I'm gettin' her number before I roll. Fuck the rides. I'm playin' hard and baggin' somethin'," Malley said, determined.

"Yeah, that's J' with the gettin' on the rides, shit," said Ka', snickering.

"No doubt," Lil J' replied, not falling for his shenanigans.

"I'm 'bout to grab some funnel cake and shoot some ball," Ka' said, cracking a smile, walking over to the basketball tent. Really, there was no lesser evil for scolding J' for wanting to get on the rides, when he wanted to play some games. The whole objective of the fair was to have fun. J' didn't pay him no mind anyway.

"I be over in a minute," Malley spoke. He was preoccupied scoping things out. J' mingled and did his thing while Ka' shot ball and Malley just drifted off into the moment. The county fair was the place to be and each year it seemed to get bigger and bigger.

"Look Ka'," said Malley, nodding his head in J's direction. He was proud that he saw J' interacting with some bad chicks. J's shyness was hot and cold when it came to bad chicks in his presence, but for some reason he was in full mack mode.

"Goddamn he done struck oil. Ay J' let me yell at you for a minute?" Ka' asked from a distance, pulling him away from the females. Kaeem wanted to find out how his lil brother pulled this one off.

"What's up? You see I'm gettin' with the shorties," J' said with confidence.

"Right, but where they from?" Kaeem questioned, very interested.

"Mt. Airy and one of 'em from West Oaklane," he responded.

"They tough, you came up," said Kaeem.

"They know we from out the "W"?" Malley asked.

"Yeah, they know. That's the first thing they asked if I was from West Philly," spoke J'.

"What's up with their friends?" Ka' asked.

"I don't know. We gotta find out," said J'.

"Yeah, I want the one in the cream. She bad as a muh'fucka. She look like she got that Indian hair," Malley stated with eagerness.

"Don't never say I ain't play my part," J' said smiling.

Malley ain't waste no time. He went and bought a big teddy bear to give to the one he liked.

"Ay sexy what's ya name?" he asked, holding the bear in his hands.

"Dominique," she said in a sweet soft voice. She had a well put together body. Malley was at a loss of words briefly, until he snapped out of his trance. He even forgot why he was holding the teddy bear for a minute.

"Here, this is for you," Malley told her, giving her the teddy bear.

"Thank you," said Dominique showing the whites of her teeth.

"Where you from?" he asked.

"West Oaklane," she replied in innocence.

"Ya man let you out this time of night?" asked Malley.

"I don't got a man. I got friends," she stated, which was sweet music to his ears.

"Hopefully you got room for another," he stated following up.

"We'll see," she responded, insinuating that there was a chance of them hooking up.

CHAPTER 31

Malley loved all the feedback she gave him. She was surely a winner. Even her girlfriends for the most part. While he laid it on her, Lil J' and Kaeem laid it on her girlfriends. It was a win-win situation for all of them. Dominique grabbed Malley's hand and wrote her number on it, telling him not to wash it off. He couldn't keep his eyes off of her glossed lips. From head to toe she was drop dead. Thoughts of holding her in his arms haunted his mind. He just imagined how soft she felt. Dominique was tougher than Simone and Turquoise but he wasn't going to trade both of his babies in for a bad chick he just met. Beauty was the norm for chicks coming from Mt. Airy and West Oaklane. After they all exchanged phone numbers, everybody went their way. Malley was still shaking his head, watching Dominique walk away switching in her tight jeans.

"J' you came through," he stated, then being interrupted by J' tapping him.

"Yo, ain't that Simone and 'em?" J' questioned staring into a pack of girls.

"Where?" Malley asked, instantly looking around, hoping she didn't see him in action. He was still recovering from the movie situation, so this would of pushed him in the hole even deeper.

"Over there." J' nodded towards the cotton candy stand.

"Aw, man we out. Hurry up. I don't want her to see me, she goin' be drawin'," stated Malley. The fair was really livening up but he didn't want to chance any unwarranted run-ins. Going undetected, they made their way out. He threw Ka' the keys so he could drive.

"Lets shoot down Billy Bobs," J' insisted.

"I got a taste for some Jims," said Ka'.

"I ain't tryna play the hood right now," Malley said, intervening.

"Yeah, you right," Ka' said, coming to his senses.

Kaeem had a mean wheel game. Him and Malley had learned how to drive around the same time. They shot down 40th Street, settled for Billy Bobs and called it a night.

After only being able to steal a few hours of sleep, Malley felt someone nudging him. He opened his eyes only to see Ka'.

"Yo, wake up," stated Ka'. Malley ignored him and rolled over.

"What, man? I'm tired, we'll catch up later on," responded Malley with his muffled voice. He tried to bury his head deeper into his pillow.

"Yo, get up man. R' just sent word."

"Yeah, what he say?" Malley asked, popping right up, but still half asleep.

"You gotta meet one of his chicks down Fridays in twenty minutes. She got somethin' for you," explained Ka'.

"Which one, down City Line Ave?" he questioned.

"Yeah."

"Alright." Malley jumped up, threw some water on his face, brushed his teeth and they took off. He didn't care that he had the same gear on from last night. It was time to make a move. Ka' drove and explained to him that one of Rod's chicks named Ameenah, would be waiting in the first booth of the non-smoking section. Malley's eyes lit up with that money glaze. A small bit of nervousness existed, but this was the point of no return in his mind. Kaeem pulled in the parking lot behind a Pathfinder. Malley got out, so he could go and handle his business. Ameenah, so beautifully awaited him sipping on a water. Her ethnicity was somewhere between asian and black. Rod sure knew how to pick them. She had her hair in a bun with a pair of Ann Klein frames on. Her attire was very conservative.

"Excuse me, R' sent me," Malley stated, hoping she was the one he was supposed to be meeting.

"Yes, I've been waitin'. My name is Ameenah," she replied, placing her hand out. Malley shook it, being polite.

"I'm Malley."

"Right, Rodney speaks highly of you."

"Yeah, that's my heart."

"The bag under the table is for you," she expressed.

"Alright," Malley said. He didn't want to grab it right away, so he ordered a water so things wouldn't seem so obvious. Ameenah finished her drink and began to stand.

"It was nice meetin' you," Amennah stated, sticking strictly to business.

"You too," he replied, respecting the loyalty she had for Rod. He grabbed the bag and walked out calmly. Ka' turned the car on once he spotted Malley coming. They blended right into traffic.

"Everythin' cool?" asked Ka', looking in the rearview mirror.

"Yeah, stop by Ez-discount when we get back down the end."

"You know the beat cops stay on the 'O,' " Ka' stated, speaking about 60th & Market.

"I gotta grab some bake & soda to cook this work up. I'm in and out," spoke Malley.

"You goin' right to work, huh?" Kaeem questioned.

"I gotta get this money, Ka'. I ain't tryin' put you under the gun, but I need you to help me with somethin'?" he asked.

"What's that?" he questioned.

"I need you to help me bag up."

"Alright," he replied.

Kaeem sparked the blunt while Malley opened the bag discovering a small package duct taped. He ripped it open seeing that Rod gave him a half a brick. Rod didn't want or expect anything back. This was a gift for him to stay on his feet and also a test to see if he could hold it down. Malley pulled out a triple beam scale and weighed up the work. Ka' watched as he mixed the bake with the coke and dropped it into the boiling water. He even dropped a couple drops of ammonia in it. This was Rod's little secret that kept the fiends coming back for more and more. Malley broke everything down into 4-½ ounces. He put sixty-two grams on each 4-½. Kaeem was amazed how it locked up when he started dropping ice cubes in the pot. He brought back an extra 9 ounces. The smell of the crack gave them both slight headaches. The windows that were open wasn't helping any. Margie impatiently waited in her room for her tester. Malley always gave out samples to get word out whenever he put a new batch on the streets.

"Ka' we gotta let it harden up," said Malley, putting the coke out on the table. Each one looked like an oversized tan cookie.

"It look hard," stated Ka'.

"The middle is still wet. We at least gotta wait like a half," stated Malley as he started cracking the 12/12 bags. The capsules was beginning to become a hassle to hide, plus the fiends wanted rocks now. A light tap on the basement door, grabbed Malley's attention. He gave Ka' the nod, grabbing his gun. Although he told Margie not to let no one in, he still didn't trust her.

"Yo . . .," said Ka'.

"It's me, y'all almost ready?" Margie asked, smelling the crack in the air, fiening for a blast.

"Alright, hold up," Malley said, breaking a chunk off of the cookie. He walked upstairs and gave her a piece.

"Thanks Malley, this better be the shit like last time," Margie stated happily.

"You know all my shit is the shit," he replied. Margie went into her room, broke a piece off and put it into her pipe. Once she fired up and took a hit, it was beam me up Scottie. By the time she exhaled the smoke, she rocked back and forth, grinding her teeth. She immediately shoved the remaining piece in her pipe and smoked it. Her eyes grew larger and her heartbeat raced. Once again Malley had some good crack. She was stuck, scratching her arms and looking around her room for things that didn't even exist. She was gone and this was good news, because if Margie liked it, so would Bobby Cool and Larry Gunther. Those were the key smokers he needed to spread the word in the hood that he had that fire. This meant that money was about to start pouring in and he was going to have 62nd Street popping.

CHAPTER 32

L ater that night Simone ended up calling Malley.
"Can I speak to Malley?" she asked.

"Yeah, what's up?" he questioned.

"Nothin', just thinkin' about you. Why you ain't call me?" she questioned.

"I was tied up somethin' serious. You know we went to see Rod," he stated.

"Oh, foreal, how he doin'?" Simone inquired.

"He good," Malley replied.

"You comin' through?" she asked.

"Probably tomorrow," said Malley.

"Well, I got a surprise for you," she stated.

"Oh yeah, what is it?" he asked, wanting to know.

"You'll see when you get here. You been to the fair yet?" questioned Simone.

"I went last night," Malley responded.

"We was there too. How many numbers you get?" she questioned, fishing for a reaction.

"Stop playin' with me. You know I only wanna be with you. Maybe I should be askin' you that question," he said, turning it right around on her.

"I ain't playin'," she responded.

"Well, we'll see. Listen, S' I gotta pick my mom up from work, so can I call you later?" he asked her.

"You better call me when you get back," she demanded.

"Alright," he stated, then hung up. He just shot some game at her. He checked in so she wouldn't be snapping on him in the morning. His real angle was to call Dominique.

"Hello? May I speak to Dominique?" he asked, not really being able to make out the voice.

"This is her, who this?" she asked.

"Malley," he replied.

"Who?" she questioned again.

"Malley," once more he replied.

"Malley? Where I know you from?" Dominique asked.

"Oh, you got amnesia already? The County Fair." He brought back to her attention.

"Oh . . . What's up? My fault," she said, coming to her senses. Malley wasn't convinced. He figured she was playing her little game.

"What's up with you, sexy?" he asked.

"I'm okay, but I could be better," replied Dominique.

"Oh yeah, how's that?" Malley inquired.

"By you keepin' me company this week," she replied.

"Oh, I can do that," said Malley, thinking with the other head.

"Well, I can't wait," she said with enthusiasm.

"Alright, I get with you then," said Malley once he saw how easy she was. It was nothing else to talk about. He lined things up, then got ready to catch up on some sleep.

"Bye," she said, before hanging up.

CHAPTER 33

The next few days he had to continue bagging up the coke. He made stack packs to put in Larry Gunther and Bobby Cool cribs and the hundred packs was for the corner hustlers. He looked out for Ka' and gave him $500 for helping him bag up. That was the least he could do. Their fingertips were blistered from burning the tips of the bags and Malley had some nicks from cutting the coke with the razors. The fiends were in soup lines waiting to be served. The youngin' s would lure them into the alleys so the cops couldn't see them when they made their rounds. The few stragglers that did have small packages didn't stand a chance with Malley having his work on the corners and in the coke spots. He allowed them to get the few loose dollars that was left.

All day long the fiends ran back and forth until they spun their last dollar. Most of the times on the first and fifteenth of the month. The undercovers knew these days were when the crack addicts would get their Welfare checks and run right to the dope dealers to spend it, so they would do whatever it took to catch them trying to score some crack. Some would dress like smokers hoping to be taken straight to the street dealers, to copp some work with marked money. Some would stakeout on the other side of Market Street in a unmarked vehicles with tinted windows, looking for transactions or some would even watch from on top of the EL, posing as Septa workers. They would go above and beyond to try to keep crack off the streets according to the law they were supposedly upholding, because some of them would even pocket some of the money. Everything wasn't always logged in and reported. A dirty cop always existed in every Police precinct. It was a game of chess being played on the streets. When it came to their surveillance, Malley was on to their tactics. His motto was catch him if you can. While 62nd Street was routinely in the swing of things, Malley was just getting home, walking through the door.

"Ay, mom . . . mom?" he yelled.

"What boy? Stop screamin' like you crazy," she replied.

"Oh, I thought you was in the other room. I got a surprise for you," he stated.

"A surprise? I know it's somethin' to this," she insinuated.

"Are you gonna be home Saturday afternoon?" asked Malley.

"I'm not sure me and your Aunt Rita are goin' shoppin'," responded his mom.

"Alright, that's cool then," he stated.

"Boy, what's the surprise?" she asked, tired of playing his games.

"I'm gonna get some things fixed up around the house for us," Malley blurted out.

"Boy . . ." She instantly tried to respond.

"Mom, I got this," he said, cutting her off. This was the first time he witnessed happiness in her eyes in a long time. She didn't justify what he was doing, but he was just trying to become the man of the house, since his dad wasn't nowhere to be found. Everything needed balance. Couldn't no single mother raise a young boy in the streets. Only a man can raise a man and he understood this.

"Jamal, I'm tellin' you, you better be careful out there," she spoke.

"Mom, I know what I'm doin'," he replied.

"I hope so. Oh, yeah some girl named Turquoise keep callin' my house all day. What her fresh behind want?" she questioned.

"Fresh? Mom you don't even know her," he said, trying to take up for her.

"You forgot I was young before. You better watch yourself, these fast ass girls," Ms. Jasmine uttered, running water over the dishes. The phone rang again. Malley picked it up.

"Hello?"

"Can I speak to Malley?" asked Turquoise.

"Yeah, what's up? Hold on. Mom, I'ma . . .," he spoke, putting the phone to his chest, looking at his mom. She had already knew it was Turquoise.

"Go ahead, I know that's your little girlfriend. We'll talk later," she stated, reading her son like a book.

"Alright, hello? Yeah, what's up?" he asked.

"You talkin' to ya girlfriend?" she asked, being sarcastic.

"You trippin'. That was my mom. I heard you was lookin' for me all day," he inquired.

"Yup, I got somethin' to tell you," she stated.

"What? What's up?" he asked.

"Guess what you gonna be?" questioned Turquoise.

"What I'm gonna be? I ain't gettin' what your implyin'," he spoke.

"You gonna be a daddy," she emphasized.

"A daddy? What? You jokin' right?" Malley asked, puzzled.

"Remember we did our thing?" she asked, reminding him.

"We only smashed once and I had a condom on," he explained in his defense.

"You know the condom broke," Turquoise said, starting to get angry.

"I ain't gonna dispute that, but maybe it's one of those false positive things," he replied, trying to wiggle his way out of reality.

"Malley, this ain't no false positive. I peed on the stick a hundred times," she said.

"How you know it's mines?" he asked.

"Don't pull that shit. This ya fuckin' baby," Turquoise spoke enraged.

"You know you been doin' ya thing, or whatever." He insinuated the possibility of the baby being someone else's.

"I ain't no hoe. This ya fuckin' baby. Be a man and the father of ya seed," she said.

"Oh I'ma sucka now, huh, Turquoise? We gettin' a test," demanded Malley.

"Fuck you Malley, you ain't shit," she responded.

"Look calm down, set up the appointment. If it's mines I'ma take care of my seed," he expressed to her. The next thing he heard was the other end of a dial tone. She hung up on him. This was bad timing. He couldn't get it through his mind how stupid he was for getting her pregnant, but then again he wore a condom. The fact that he was making his mom an early grandmother didn't bother him. He was worrying about Simone and Ms. Maxine telling him not to hurt her daughter. He drove up to Simone's house to spend some time with her. Simone and her girlfriend Tracey were sitting on the steps when he pulled up.

"S' what's up baby?" he asked, as he sat in the car.

"Ain't no what's up baby," she replied, trying to play hard ball in front of Tracey.

"Come here, stop playin' all the time. Why you frontin'?" he questioned, leaning back in his seat. She got up off the steps making her way over to the car, giving him a peck on the lips.

"What's up?" she asked.

"Take this ride with me," he invited.

"Alright Tracey I see you later. I got somethin' to tell you," she stated, then they pulled off.

"What's wrong?" he asked, noticing her long face.

"Remember that surprise I said I had for you?" she asked.

"Yeah, surprises don't call for sad faces though," he spoke.

"Just promise me . . .," Simone stated, as her eyes began to water.

"Promise you what? What's wrong?" he asked, pulling over.

"Malley I've been throwin' up a lot lately," Simone conveyed.

"You alright? You ain't dyin' on me is you?" he asked, trying to add a little humor.

"Stop playin'. This is serious," she stated.

"Alright, give me the surprise that's so serious," asked Malley.

"I went to the hospital yesterday for a checkup and my doctor told me I was pregnant," said Simone.

"Huh? Pregnant? You serious?" Malley's entire body went numb. All he heard was his heart beating. Deja vu struck again.

"Yeah, I'm pregnant," she said, with a serious face.

"Your miz know yet?" he questioned, scratching his head.

"Yeah, she think you're not gonna be there for me," Simone said.

"She said that?" he asked, shocked.

"Yup, she's just off balance right now," Simone stated, protecting her mom.

"I hope so because you know how I feel about you." He just said that to lower any inclination that he wouldn't be there for her. In the back of his mind he didn't know what he was going to do. Simone had a good head on her shoulders and she came from a good family. He chose not to run from facing his new responsibility. He drove home to let Simone meet his mother and break the news. This was the inevitable. It had to be addressed. A million and one insecurities ran through Simone's mind. She was worried if Malley's mother was going to accept her or not.

CHAPTER 34

Ms. Jasmine must have had stepped out for a minute because when she walked through the door Malley and Simone were sitting on the couch. She appeared to be shocked. Malley had never brought a female home before, waiting to meet his mother.

"Hey mom?" He greeted her with a kiss on the cheek.

"And who are you?" she asked, not paying Malley any mind.

"Mom that's . . .," Malley said, trying to explain before he was cut off.

"I didn't ask you. I asked her," Ms. Jasmine replied.

"My name is Simone," she responded.

"So you just bring company over when you want now?" Ms. Jasmine asked.

"Naw, mom it ain't that. I gotta tell you somethin'," he said.

"Boy I know you ain't got this girl pregnant?" she questioned, seeing right through the situation.

"I told you she wouldn't like me," Simone blurted out, storming for the door.

"Wait, wait, wait, mom . . .," Malley said, stopping Simone from leaving. She broke down crying as she felt embarrassed. Malley put his arms around her so that she could feel a state of ease.

"I'm sorry baby. I overacted, it's just the two of you are so young to be havin' a baby. It's a lot of responsibilities," Ms. Jasmine stated, reminiscing when she first got pregnant with Jamal.

"I know mom," he said.

"Oh no you don't. Pampers, milk, warm bottles, clothes, the baby wakin' up in the middle of the night. You don't know," she insisted, schooling him.

"Mom, I'ma do what I gotta, to be there for her," he reiterated.

"Listen to you. You still live home with me. Anyway baby what's your name again?" she questioned.

"Simone," she responded with watery eyes.

"Mines is Jasmine, but call me Ms. Jazzy, okay?" she said, making it clear.

"Umm-hmm," Simone replied, nodding her head in agreement.

"So Jamal, since you're makin' shoes for the feet, do her mom know?" she asked.

"She know," Simone stated, intervening.

"Okay, well I think me and her should have a talk, so me and her can be on one accord," Ms. Jasmine explained. The thought of Ms. Jasmine becoming a grandmother some day was well on her wish list, but this was too soon. Any insinuation of having an abortion was out the question. Ms. Jasmine was old school when it came to that. Now Simone's mother take on things was another story and Ms. Jasmine wanted to get to the bottom of it. Simone felt accepted after talking to Ms. Jasmine. The next step for Malley was to face Ms. Maxine with the pregnancy.

Later on that night Malley had found out that the jammie boys had stuck up two of his workers for $500 and the jump outs ran in Bobby Cool's house and took $1,000 in money and coke. He had just took two losses. The plot was beginning to thicken. These were the evils of the game Rod warned him of. With the pressure of having Simone and Turquoise pregnant at the same time without them both knowing and the fact that Rod was facing life was taking a toll on him. He now had to find out who robbed his workers because if he didn't do nothing or at least investigate, it's no doubt the stick up boys would be back for more. He needed to give the youngin's out on the corners .25 automatics to keep the wolves away when they would try another attempt of robbery. The lost at Bobby Cool's had to be charged to the game. It was the cops and that's what they do. All he could do was wait for things to die down and open shop back up. The streets was talking and dudes were jealous as Malley's name started to ring.

CHAPTER 35

Within three weeks of summer going by. Everything hit Malley all at once. He laid low to try to keep an eye on his new found enemies. Now it seemed like every time he turned around, he was taking money out of his pocket for something. If it wasn't parts for his mechanic to put on his cars, it was the stash he was building to prepare for his two babies that were on the way. At times he would second guess himself thinking that he may have been way in over his head, but every time his pride told him otherwise. This game came with non-stop responsibilities and the most important one was staying on his toes at all times. Keeping the pregnancy of Turquoise a secret from his mom didn't sit right with him, it was stressing him out not to tell her. He had to tell her as reality was smacking him dead in the face. Nobody knows their child better than the parent themselves. She could tell that he wanted to say something to her all day, but hesitated.

"Now what's wrong? Them streets wearin' you down, huh?" she questioned.

"Man . . .," he said, not finishing his thought.

"You're gonna have to slow down, bein' you have a child on the way," she expressed.

"I know . . .," responded Malley.

"I'm serious, it's not about just you no more," Ms. Jasmine said sternly.

"Mom . . . you ain't gonna believe this," he said.

"What?" she asked.

"I got another girl pregnant too. At least that's what she's sayin'," he stated.

"Boy have you lost your goddamn mind? Hello? Is anybody home?" she asked, knocking on his head with a closed fist. Malley stood there with the puppy dog face.

"I just . . .," he spoke, not finishing his sentence.

"You're just havin' a good ol' time, huh? What's her name?" she questioned sarcastically.

"Turquoise," he spoke.

"That fresh ass girl who was calling my house? Where she live at?" Ms. Jasmine questioned.

"Wynnefield," Malley stated.

"So you was just gonna bring her in here with a big stomach like you did Simone?" asked Ms. Jasmine.

"Mom that's not how it was supposed to be," he said, trying to plead his case.

"Don't give me that shit. I told you time after time to protect yourself. And you shouldn't be havin' sex anyway. You better get ready for school in a few months," she said in anger, pulling on her Newport, watching the fire turn orange.

"I'ma be ready," he stated.

"Do Simone know you got this other girl pregnant? Never mind don't answer that," she ranted.

"They sort of know each other," he explained.

"Boy is you crazy? You ain't gonna stress me the hell out," she stated. Malley had to break the news to her. The situation he was in couldn't be undone. All he could do was embrace it. Malley called it a night to get ready to go to Rod's trial.

The Federal Building was swarming with news reporters and other media press. The people Rod was aligned with, brought some attention to who he was. Everyone remained seated as the US Marshals brought him into the courtroom. Malley was in high spirits after seeing his old head. He kept tapping Kaeem on the side. He was ecstatic just as well. His Aunt Rita was also there showing her support. His mom couldn't take off work, so she sent her love and blessings.

"Look they bringin' him out" said Malley.

"Yeah, I know," spoke Kaeem. Rod saw the family support. A few of the woman he were dating showed up in his honor. This was something new and boring to Malley. The U.S Attorney presented witness after witness who were cooperating against Rod. His lawyers immediately attacked the turncoat witnesses credibility, hoping to convince the jury that they were just using Rod as an escape goat to minimize their participation. This was only a ploy to lessen up their sentence as much as possible or even have an opportunity to walk. The first day dragged and dragged and Malley couldn't wait to get out of there. Trial was finally adjourned for the day and the jurors were dismissed. The judge allowed them a quick family interaction.

After they got back in the neighborhood, Malley decided that he didn't want to be seen and wanted to go check out Turquoise. Him and Kaeem took 59th Street straight up. The streets were empty this night until he got to 59th & Thompson. He could see the corner of 59th & Master was packed with street hustlers and other soldiers who gambled on the side of the Blue Velvet bar. As the car came to a stop, Malley hit the horn at a few players he knew out there. No soon as he pulled off, shots rang out; POP . . . POP . . . POP! The back window shattered instantly, sending pieces of glass throughout the car.

"What the fuck?!" Malley questioned, as he ducked down, stepping on the gas.

"Yo, they cuttin' on us," said Kaeem with his head low looking in the rearview mirror. The figure of the shooter who stood in the middle of the street got smaller as they pulled further away. The car tires screeched as Malley made a hard left on 59th & Media. All he was trying to do was get out of harms reach.

"Yo you see who it was?" Malley asked, with his adrenaline racing.

"Naw, but we gotta bark at D' and 'em to see what's what," Kaeem insisted.

"Yeah," Malley said convinced.

"You think it was somebody from Master Street?" Ka' questioned.

"Naw, they peoples. It had to be somebody out there at the crap game," Malley implied. He knew everybody from 59th to 56th & Master from going to Shoemaker and he was cool with all of them, so he ruled them out. This came from somebody else and he was going find out.

"So what's next?" Kaeem asked.

"Niggaz tried to bang me, it's on," Malley said, parking that car and jumping into another one, then dropping Kaeem off. The fact that somebody had just shot at him had him uptight. He needed to find out where it came from. Malley wanted to get his hands on some more heat. The .380 he had didn't make him feel safe. He still drove up to Turquoise's that night. The feeling of flirting with danger boosted his heart even more, after he calmed himself. He kept his .380 in arms reach in case he had to fire at will. At this point his choice of trusting anybody outside of Ka' and Lil J' was slim to none, especially until he was able to discover who shot at him and why. Each car that drove by or had tinted windows had him on pins and needles. Even when the cops would drive by he would panic. He leaned against his car with his hands in his hoodie, clutching his gun as he spoke with Turquoise. If the culprits were still looking for him he was definitely ready this time.

"I gotta put you on to somethin'," he explained.

"What?" Turquoise asked, quickly being newsy.

"Man . . . shh. Yo, I don't need you trippin', just chill," he said.

"Chill about what?" she asked again.

"I got another baby on the way," he stated, just spitting it out.

"What?! Ooh, no you didn't. It better not be that bitch. Tell me it's her and I'ma kick her right in her stomach," she replied in anger.

"I told you to chill," stated Malley.

"Ah, unn . . . she ain't havin' no baby by you," she replied.

"You got niggaz you be dealin' with," he told her flat out.

"So what pussy, you know this ya baby," she said with one hand on her hip and the other pointing in his face.

"You better watch your mouth and get your hands outta my face. Just calm down, we goin' work this shit out," he informed her.

"Ooh . . . I'ma kick her ass!" she said with authority. The worst thing he could of done was start a war between two baby mothers. This was past a cat fight and the fire was too big to put out. Things continued to come at Malley at a rapid pace and this is what the fast lane cultivated. Malley had chose this way of life, so now it was his task to find out how to deal with it.

CHAPTER 36

Rod's trial continued to get uglier and uglier. Evidence just kept pouring from out of nowhere. They mainly had him on audio. Rod barley spoke on phones so the Feds had their agents wear wires to get the conversations they needed. They were aware of all the major players he was serving. The likelihood of Rod getting acquitted was wearing very thin. Malley still kept his ears open during the trial, not knowing if the Feds knew that Rod supplied him, or if they had enough evidence and just didn't care. This was a smart way to think because when it comes to the Federal Government they relinquish any and all remorse of age or gender when violations of the R.I.C.O., CCE or other criminal statues are broken. The Feds don't waste their time so when they come, they got all that they need for their indictment.

Malley done his homework and got with his hommie D' from 59th & Master to find out who shot at him the other night. Word was that it was the bol Tae from 60th & Girard. Him and Malley had exchanged words down club Dances and anytime they would see each other they would just lock eyes with dirty looks, but nothing never happened until that night. Tae had a lot of heart, most people from his hood was scared of him. He was like the only young buck from around his way that played with guns his age. He hustled, gambled and took money. He was already in and out of placements. He ran from Sleighton Farms and St. Gabrielle Hall when he got his home passes. Malley linked back up with Ka'. He was fuming once he found out who shot at him. He had to strike back. Tae was the big mouth type and knew he probably was bragging about what he done.

"Yo you know I got word, who chopped on us," spoke Malley.

"Yeah, who?" Ka' asked.

"The bol Tae," said Malley.

"Tae, Tae, Tae," he said pondering.

"Tae, the nigga from the 60th & Girard," he blurted out.

"Yeah, what's that about?" Kaeem inquired.

"Me and bol had words down Dances last month. And every time we see each other we get to grittin!" said Malley.

"Oh, bol on some jealous shit, huh?" Kaeem asked.

"He heard I'm gettin' to a dollar, plus his B.M. on my dick. She want me to fuck but I ain't get around to it yet," Malley said being cocky.

"Yeah, so this shit about you gettin' money and a chick?" Kaeem questioned.

"Yeah. You know dude just came home, so he out here runnin' wild tryin' to put fear in niggaz," spoke Malley.

"Dude could of killed us," said Kaeem.

"I'ma get at dude. Ka' I don't need you involved in this," Malley proclaimed.

"He ain't just shoot at you. You forgot I was in the car too?" Kaeem questioned.

"Alright, listen all I need you to do is drive the wheel. I'ma do the squeezin'," Malley emphasized.

Kaeem was getting sucked in. This wasn't even his forte. Kaeem was into playing basketball but hanging around his cousin was influencing his actions and now becoming a habit.

"Mal, you're like my real brother, ain't nothin' gonna happen to you," Kaeem stated, displaying his loyalty.

"Ka' I luv you, man," Malley expressed.

"Nigga we family," Kaeem replied.

Nightfall was present and it was time to try to strike back. Tae and the rest of the bols from up there would usually be standing out in front of the Chinese store or the State store. About five bols was out there when they were approaching 60th & Girard. Malley told Ka' to drive by first so he could make sure that Tae was out there. They drove by unnoticed as Tae leaned against the Chinese store wall, talking to his homies.

"Yo I think that's him," spoke Kaeem.

"Yeah, that was him," responded Malley, turning his .380 from side to side, getting ready to unload. Kaeem drove up Edgewood Street. Tae and his homies would be unprepared with them turning right off of the block. As they got to the middle of the block, Malley's heart started to trot. He rolled the window down and gave Kaeem the signal. Kaeem turned the corner and they were still out there, lunching. Malley just stuck his arm out the window and let loose; POP . . . POP . . . POP . . . POP . . . POP . . . POP . . . POP! Everybody ran for cover. The shots put holes in the Chinese store window and the abandoned house next to it. He wasn't sure if he shot Tae nor anybody who was out there, or was he sticking around to find out. But he knew he let all seven shots go. Kaeem drove all the way up 55th & Girard, then turned back towards Vine Street.

"Yeah we cut on them chumps," said Malley, feeling a sense of relief. Kaeem looked as if he felt some contentment also. Malley sent a message that if anybody was going to try him, that there would be repercussions. They ditched the car and Kaeem took him to Simone's. As soon as he got there he got into a petty argument with her.

"Oh, you just come and go when you please? I'm tired of ya shit," Simone stated.

"I'm tired and you trippin' for nothin'," Malley spat.

"Ain't no, I'm trippin'. Where was you at?" she asked aggravated.

"You ain't my mom," he replied.

"That's right I'm your girl and I'm about to have ya baby," she responded.

"S' you know I be makin' moves. You gotta chill. That's that pregnant shit talkin'," said Malley.

"I don't want to hear that," Simone replied.

"Alright, whatever," he said. Kaeem had took the wheel so he had to wait for him to pick him up in the morning. Malley put the pillow over his head and went to sleep. He left early in the morning before Simone got up. He found himself playing tennis between her and Turquoise. Depending on their mood swings, dictated who he spent time with. Next stop was Turquoise's.

"Come in, what that bitch kicked you out?" she asked, letting him in the house.

"Oh, you too, huh?" he asked, thinking he escaped the bickering.

"Whatever, you and her goin' through, don't bring it here," spoke Turquoise. He just shook his head. He knew she just wanted to be number one. He gave her what she wanted—some attention and piped her down good, putting her right to sleep.

CHAPTER 37

Rod's trial had came to a conclusion and the jury had finished deliberations. Once again the courtroom was filled with spectators. Malley, Kaeem, Lil J' and Ms. Rita sat behind the defense table. The foreman returned with an unreadable face. This was the moment everyone was waiting for. The U.S. Marshal handed the verdict sheet to the judge, in turn he instructed for Rod to stand. Rod stood with confidence next to his defense team. He looked back at his family, winked at Malley, then turned back around.

"In the indictment of Rodney Robinson as to running a Corrupt Organization how do you find?" the judge asked.

"Guilty," the foreman announced.

"That's bullshit," Malley blurted out.

"Calm down Jamal," his Aunt Rita stated.

"That's crazy," said Kaeem.

"Man . . .," Lil J' said, weighing in, not finishing his thoughts.

"Each of you young men will be quiet in my courtroom," the judge emphasized.

"It won't happen again Your Honor," Ms. Rita stated.

"In the indictment of Rodney Robinson as to distributing large quantities of cocaine to Federal informants. How do you find?" the judge asked.

"Guilty," the foreman announced again.

"Man . . . fuck this courtroom!" Malley said, standing up belligerent. Hearing that Rod was found guilty, hurt him to his heart. The judge immediately addressed him.

"That's enough young man. Remove him from my courtroom now," the judge ordered furiously. The U.S. Marshals restrained Malley, dragging him out of the courtroom.

"Where are you taking him?" Ms. Rita asked one of the Marshals.

"Just outside Ma'am," he responded, continuing his order. Her eyes begin to mist up at the sight of her nephew meeting defeat. Kaeem and Lil J' comforted their mother, showing strength.

"In the third indictment of Rodney Robinson as to commit conspiracy to transport twenty kilos of cocaine through Florida to Philadelphia. How do you find?" the judge asked.

"Guilty," the foreman continued to announce.

"Is this your final verdict?" questioned the judge.

"Yes Your Honor," the foreman responded.

"Thank you ladies and gentlemen of the jury. You may leave through that door. Mr. Scott does your client have anything to say before sentencing is imposed?" the judge asked.

"Yeah, I got somethin' to say. Fuck you and this crooked ass judicial system. All you is, is a coward in a black robe with no balls," Rod said, remaining firm. He wasn't going to let his family see him crumble into a million pieces. The judge was taken aback at Rod's response.

"You're . . . you're hereby sentenced to 180 months for the first indictment and your last indictment, raises above the kingpin statue, which you're to serve life in Federal custody. You may appeal this judgment and sentence within thirty days. Now get out of my courtroom and don't think about a reconsideration, you scum bag," the judge stated, exasperated.

"I be back on appeal," Rod said with confidence as the U.S. Marshals took him to his holding cell.

"It's alright mom," said Kaeem, handing her a facial tissue as they begin to leave. Malley's eyes grew big watching them come out of the courtroom.

"Lil J', what's what?" Malley asked, wondering why his head was to the ground.

"Man, they gave him life," J' told him.

"They did what?!" Malley questioned in disbelief.

"Jamal they gave him life," spoke his Aunt Rita. Malley placed both hands on top of his head trying to bear the bad news.

Rod ended up paying his lawyers over $75,000 a piece. Spending all that money got him nothing but a life sentence. Malley felt as though the lawyers sold him out and that the courts railroaded his old head. So he was going to do everything he could to see his family on the streets again. His Aunt Rita drove them to the Federal building where Rod was being held, so they could see him before he was sent away. The C.O.'s brought him right out, but he had to get his visit behind the glass because he was sentenced already. The Feds never took chances on sentenced inmates. Malley picked up the phone, staring Rod in his eyes.

"What's up ol'head?" Malley asked, depressed.

"I'm chillin'," he replied, maintaining his composure.

"They railroaded you," said Malley.

"I know youngin'. That's how bad they wanted me. I'll be back, my money too long," Rod stated, instilling hope.

"R' somethin' gotta be done. What's up with ya appeal?" asked Malley, concerned with his options.

"Donna is gonna retain the lawyers for me this week. Look, I'ma be bouncin' around from state to state until I get classified. So I'll get word to you when I get situated," he explained to him.

"R' you ain't doin' no life, you comin' home," said Malley with confidence.

"I feel you. Look you, Ka' and J' gotta take care of the family," spoke Rod. Malley knew exactly what he meant. This was a subliminal message telling him that the salons and barbershops was now his. Malley also knew that the Feds didn't get everything. Rod had stash spots all over and most likely something else was coming his way.

"No doubt," Malley responded.

"Let me speak to auntie before she have a heart attack," he said, cutting things short.

"Yeah, we wouldn't want that," he replied, cracking a smirk.

"Alright, man, I luv you youngin'," Rod said, putting his fist up to the glass.

"I luv you too," Malley responded, putting his fist up as well, before getting up. Seeing his old head in this tragic predicament had him distraught, but he had to keep living his life. He vowed to make sure he wouldn't want for anything as long as he was out on the streets. Rod had became another casualty of war from the betrayal of other players he trusted in the game and an unethical judicial system.

CHAPTER 38

Malley took care of what he was asked. He stayed on top of the lawyers to make sure they got their money and that Rod's appeal was being filed. Him and Simone was still on the outs. Her and Kaeem had begun to build a nice rapport and would communicate from time to time. If anything, Malley needed him to try and patch things over between them, because the ditch he dug was getting deeper and deeper. Kaeem picked up his phone after it rang three times.

"Hello?" he answered.

"Can I speak to Kaeem?" Simone asked.

"Yeah, who this?" he asked.

"It's Si . . . mone," she stated, stammering in a troubled voice.

"S', what's wrong?" he questioned concerned.

"I'ma . . . I'ma . . ." she stated, trying to get her words out.

"Slow down, slow down," he told her.

"I'ma . . . kill him and her," she said emotionally.

"Hold up, ya talkin' crazy right now. What's wrong?" he asked again.

"He got me and that bitch pregnant," she finally blurted out.

"What?"   How you know that?" Kaeem questioned.

"Because Kaeem, she mailed the paternity test to my house. I know she done it. She tryin' be spiteful," she expressed.

"That sound kind of . . ." he said, before being cut off.

"Kind of what?   I can read. I know what a real paternity test look like. He could of at least told me. I'm stressin'. I can't eat or nothin'," Simone explained to him.

"You gotta eat somethin'. You can't starve the baby." The reality of the situation was beginning to settle in. Malley was now in a deep mess and it was pretty much too late to try and clean it up.

"Kaeem, I don't know what I'm gonna do. I luv him, how could he do somethin' like this to me?" she questioned.

"We gonna get to the bottom of this, so don't panic," Kaeem said, trying to keep her calm. He talked her into letting him speak with Malley about the latest news.

After they hung up, Kaeem called Malley immediately.

"Yo, Mal?" spoke Kaeem.

"Who this?" he asked.

"You don't know ya cousin voice by now?" said Kaeem.

"Naw, it ain't that. I just smoked a blunt. I'm on right now," he stated.

"You know S' know?" he questioned.

"Know what?" he asked, unaware.

"I just got off the phone with her and she said Turquoise sent her the paternity test," Kaeem informed him.

"What?! She did what?!" asked Malley, shocked.

"Yeah, true story," he said.

"What the fuck is wrong with that broad?" he asked in disgust.

"Mal, you in some shit," Kaeem stated.

"I know. Fuck it now, we ain't gettin' no abortions," Malley said.

"She say she luv you man," he expressed.

"Ka' I don't doubt that. I'm 'bout to roll some more weed up," Malley stated.

"Alright, I get with you in the a.m.," Kaeem spoke, then hung up.

Malley wanted to go into a zone. He needed some time by himself. No music, no chicks, no nothing, just his thoughts. The Simone and Turquoise dilemma seemed to fester by the day. Turquoise just upped the anti by throwing her pregnancy in Simone's face. This was a ploy to make her jealous and it was surely working. Malley wanted to salvage his relationship with Simone, but still wanted Turquoise in his life. He made his way over to her house to confront her about her actions.

"Don't be bangin' on my door like that," Turquoise said upon opening it.

"Why you do that nut shit?" he inquired.

"What? I don't know what ya talkin' 'bout," she replied.

"Oh, you wanna play dumb, now? That's why I hate dealin' with you nut ass chicks. Why you send Simone the paternity test?" he asked, pissed.

"Because I wanted to. You belong to me, not her. What she want some problems?" she questioned sarcastically.

"You ain't in her league on the brawlin' side of things. She'll trash you," he told her.

"Yeah, right. I'm havin' ya baby, rather she like it or not," she said, affirming her decision.

"Look, I ain't got time for y'all nut ass games. One of y'all better grow up quick," he explained.

"You know I luv you boy. I'm just scared to lose you," she said, kissing him on his neck as he heard those words all before.

"Chill . . .," he said, trying to resist her seduction.

"You know you want this wet pregnant pussy," Turquoise stated, putting his hand in her panties. Her warm and moist juices lathered his fingers, giving him an instant hard on. Once again he found himself tangled in Charlotte's Web. Before he knew it, his pants were down around his ankles and he found himself on top of Turquoise, humping away. Denying the fact that he loved both of his soon to be baby mothers was too evident to dismiss. He didn't have an answer nor knew how things were going to play out. He was just along for the ride.

CHAPTER 39

Rod was out in Kansas still being shipped around awaiting to be classified to his jail. The lawyers had begun reviewing his notes of testimony for errors to see if he had any grounds for a new trial. Things were somewhat quiet after Malley shot at Tae. But he figured he probably would be planning a retaliation sooner or later, so he kept his eyes open just in case. The salons and barbershops stayed in tact, while he maintained his running around. Kaeem had informed Malley that he saw Tae with one of his gunslingers down the Clam Bar, spitting game at some chicks, but they didn't see him. Malley entertained the news, then kept in tune with his daily routine. Later that night, Tae and a few of his henchmen ran down on 62nd Street. They jammed the crap game and whomever was out there working for Malley. Tae made sure that he shot one of the workers in the leg to let Malley know that it was on and popping. This was something to be expected as Tae had a reputation of not letting things go, so backing down wasn't even a thought in his mind.

After Malley found out about the retaliation it dawned on him that Tae was going to be a problem. The streets had heard of the latest attack and awaited

Malley's reaction. He had now entered into a game of chess and he couldn't squander the first chance at some get back. Going back up 60th & Girard, shooting the corner up again was an idea, but the objective was to get his target and Malley didn't want to hit an innocent bystander, let alone shoot Tae. The game was forcing him to play with guns, turning him cold-hearted. This was the only way to keep the gorillas off his back. Respect had to be demanded if he wanted to be taken serious out in the jungle.

Malley had the utmost respect for his mom. They had the type of relationship that he could talk to her almost about anything. She always gave him the best advice a mother could give her son. The double pregnancy weighed heavy on his mind, although he was moving fast in the streets, he was still a teenager. He adhered to the basics of never hitting women and taking care of a child if you made one. Being a man came with many responsibilities and these were just two attributes.

"What's wrong?" Malley's mom asked, noticing a sign worry across his face.

"Ain't nothin' wrong," he replied, trying to throw her off.

"You're my son, I brought you in this world. I know when somethin's wrong with my child," she enforced.

"Naw, I'm just stressin' a lil. Turquoise and Simone is drivin' me crazy," he replied.

"Baby that's somethin' you have to deal with. You chose to lay down with those two girls, now it's time to be a man. But, I'ma let you know this is just the beginnin' of it," his mom said, setting him straight.

"Mom, I'm thinkin' about gettin' an apartment," said Malley.

"That's good, but how are you gonna work that out?" she asked.

"Work what out?" he questioned back.

"Both of those girls certainly can't stay with you, so who's stayin' with you?" she asked, wanting to know.

"I don't know. I guess Simone," he said, uncertain.

"Well, that's somethin' to consider," she stated.

"Right, right," he responded. Receiving her motherly support always put him at ease.

Kaeem convinced Malley to go out Saturday night. Club Dances was always the place to be on the weekends. People from allover would come, just to say that they were there, or either the Lumber Jack. These were just those types of clubs. And this night Malley looked forward to a little excitement. The line was packed as the patrons awaited to be searched by the bouncers. The music pounded from the speakers finding it's way onto the streets as Kaeem and Malley were being searched. As they entered, the florescent lights waved on and off of the girls dancing on the dance floor. Malley and Kaeem made their way in the cut, to be able to peep the scene out. The DJ made brief intermissions, hyping up the party over Naughty by Nature's: O.P.P.

"You down with O.P.P?" the DJ yelled, followed by; "Yeah you know me." The crowd responded back in unison. The DJ continued to play anthem after anthem as the night moved along. Malley and Kaeem wasn't really the dancing type, so they just played the wall and let the girls grind up against them. This night the whole 29th & Allegheny was in Dances and they were on the prowl for trouble. Malley's name often found its way across the city through word of mouth. Everyone who wasn't with the Allegheny squad saw how they were walking around like they owned the joint. They were only out just to take the edge off, but trouble would soon find them. The heart of their squad walked past Malley, bumping him on purpose.

"Yo, what's up? Watch where you goin'," Malley replied to his intentional clash.

"What? Watch where I'm goin'," Scoop replied, walking towards Malley.

"Yo, everythin' cool," Kaeem stated, jumping in between the both of them.

"Naw, everythin' ain't cool," Scoop replied, staring Malley dead in his eyes.

"You heard what I said, watch where you're goin'," Malley responded.

"Nigga, my name Scoop. I'm from 29th Street," he told him.

"Yeah, and my name Malley. I'm from 62nd Street. My heart don't pump no Kool-Aid," he spat right back.

"Come on Mal, we out," spoke Kaeem. The bouncers observed the heated standoff and kicked both parties out as the spectators anticipated some action. Malley was in his feelings, making his way to the car. He didn't like the fact of Scoop bumping him for no reason.

"Man, that was corny," stated Kaeem.

"Them dudes is suckas. Man, I don't even know main man and them," Malley said.

"Jealously," spoke Kaeem. Something told them to turn around on their way to the car. Scoop and his entourage were following them.

"What's up? You goin' give me a rumble," said Scoop, pointing at Malley.

"Yeah, we goin' rumble all y'all. Line that shit up," he responded immediately.

"Where you goin'?" asked Scoop, watching Malley open his car door.

"We goin' give y'all a rumble," Malley spoke as he reached underneath his seat, pulling out a black 9mm. Scoop's eyes contorted as he saw Malley brandish the gun. He quickly did an about face and took off, which he felt like he was running in slow motion. Without thought, Malley fired at him; BLOC . . . BLOC . . . BLOC . . . BLOC . . . BLOC . . . BLOC! was the sound of the shots roaring as the shells found their way on the pavement. Scoops entourage took off with him like a bat out of hell. Kaeem and Malley quickly jumped in the car and sped off. He must of ran like three lights trying to get back home.

"Oh, shit, you think you hit him?" Kaeem asked.

"I don't know, but fuck 'em they came at us," Malley replied, with his adrenaline pumping. Things seemed harder for Kaeem to escape, every time he turned around he was into some craziness with Malley. His basketball days appeared to be withering away. Malley trusted Lil J' but having Kaeem being his eyes was enough already.

"Shit is crazy out here," Kaeem spoke.

"I know and the crazy thing is, you can't get money and go to war," Malley explained to him driving past 30th Street station.

CHAPTER 40

A few weeks after the shoot-outs, Malley just kept playing things by ear. Only a fool would go back out to party while things were heated between the two now rivals. Money continued to come in and joggling time between Simone and Turquoise was still a hassle. He finally brought an apartment up Upper Darby that he shared with Simone. This was a low key spot for him. He got his mom to buy it for him to lower any type suspicion. Simone stood at the stove, preparing dinner. Baked macaroni and cheese and fried chicken was on the menu. The smell of the food reminded him of his mom's cooking. Simone had learned from her mom. Inheriting her mothers beauty wasn't the only thing about her. Malley laid on the couch waiting to devour one of her plates, also with thoughts of having her for dessert. Her derriere filled out each inch of her booty shorts. Every time she walked from the refrigerator to the stove, Malley's eyes permanently admired Simone's stature. The phone rang, grabbing his attention. He shook his head before answering.

"Hello?" he asked.

"You have a collect call from . . . R' from a Federal institution. This call will be monitored and recorded.

To accept this call press 5 now," the operator explained. Malley quickly accepted.

"Hello?" Rod questioned as he wasn't able to hear anything.

"Yo, yo, I'm here," stated Malley.

"What's up bol?" Rod asked.

"Maintainin'. What's up with the lawyers?" Malley asked eagerly.

"They said I got some good issues for my appeal," Rod shared, restoring hope.

"Is they goin' get the job done?" he questioned.

"Hopefully, we gotta see how the courts play, but I got some good issues," spoke Rod.

"Damn man, I miss you. I wish you was out here," Malley emphasized.

"Yeah, I know. I be there in a minute," he replied.

"I'm thinkin' 'bout takin' a trip," Malley told him. Rod already heard about the couple squabbles he had, so he knew that he was telling him he was laying low.

"Yeah do that. You gotta take a trip here and there. How's Simone and Turquoise doin'?" he asked being smart.

"They still gang warrin'. PMS, pregnancy and jealousy is a crazy mixture. I don't know what I got myself into, but me and Simone layin' up together," he explained to him.

"Okay playa. I see you took heed to my advice," Rod stated, recognizing how Malley implemented a jewel he dropped on him.

"Yeah, Simone more grounded," Malley responded.

"What you say boy?" Simone asked, hearing her name.

"Nothin'. Chill. Yeah you was right. So where you at?" he asked.

"I'm at Allenwood, but it ain't no tellin' where I'ma be at next," Rod stated before the operator interrupted their conversation stating Rod had only one minute left.

"Damn, they just interrupt when they want, huh?" he asked, absolutely naïve to the penal system.

"Somethin' like that. Look, make sure you stay focused out there and I'ma call back soon," he said.

"You have 15 seconds left," the operator announced.

"Alright ol'head. I luv you man. Keep ya head up, you be home soon," Malley said, speaking from the heart.

"No doubt," Rod replied as the phone went dead. He looked at it hoping Malley heard him.

All Malley heard was what he said before they got cut off. Even though he wished he could talk longer, he was elated to just hear from him. Simone walked over to him with his plate, sitting next to him.

"Damn, babe I miss my ol'head," he expressed.

"Don't worry he'll be home soon," she said, comforting him. Hearing that made him feel kind of better after alluding his last two run-ins.

While everything was going on, Kaeem got back on track with playing ball. He played for Sonny Hill and Press On. Sometimes they would have to play PAL and the Salvation Army League. He frequented from Haddington's to Cobbscreek, when he wanted to practice. Helping his cousin was out of sheer loyalty. Being a basketball star someday was his dream. He looked up to Dr. J' as he could remember his dad taking him to the Spectrum to see the Sixers play when he was a kid. Lil J' came out to support his brother every chance he got, whether he was practicing or playing in an actual game. Malley played his position, continuing to lay low. Things had to blow over before it would be a good idea for him to play the hood in the daytime full-blown. Nobody knew that Kaeem was with him on both of the shootings, not even J', so he was okay. The day was winding down and for some reason Cobbscreek was empty. Only the recreation manager, two other ballers running roc and Kaeem and J' were present. Lil J' passed him the ball as he squared up to shoot a jump shot. The first one rimmed out, so he passed him another one and this time it went straight in.

"Yo bro, Malley out here trippin'," said J', passing him the ball again.

"Yeah, he doin' what he do," replied Kaeem, bouncing the ball.

"You know we gotta stay focused. The streets isn't for us. You remember how much Rod used to beat in our head to stay away from it," said J'.

"Yeah, I know," Kaeem replied, but thinking to himself if Lil J' only knew.

"Not just me and you, Malley too," J' stated.

"I know. He just tryin' make a couple dollars. He ain't in it too long," Kaeem spoke, shooting another jump shot, this time missing.

"Stay in it too long? Ka' we played the look-outs when he first started hustlin'. He made some change, now he really rippin' it. What he want out of it? What he tryin' to get knocked?" J' asked, not understanding why Malley was still hustling after he had came up already.

"J', he know what he doin'," Kaeem replied, knowing that Malley didn't have any intentions on stopping no time soon.

"I hope so. He got two babies on the way," J' replied, grabbing the ball taking a shot at the rim.

CHAPTER 41

Malley showed his face in the hood only at nighttime. This was one of his ways of maneuvering to check on Bobby Cool and Larry Gunther's and at the same time staying in the trenches. These were his main two cash-cows, so making sure his product stayed flowing would assure that his money continued to come in. Dressed down in black Dickie sets was his attire. Nobody was familiar with his tinted, blue Corsica he drove. Switching his cars was the norm, especially after the shoot-outs. As he dipped in and out of both spots he kept a .9mm on his hip. The fiends found their way into either house hoping to score. Malley stood in the dinning room of Bobby Cool's with his gun in hand, while his young bol served the fiends who came in and out, or those who decided to stay. The fiends felt comfortable spending money in smokehouses because these were environments that enabled them to get high in private and without any worries of being robbed. Larry Gunther's brought in a nice bankroll but Bobby Cool's would always produce the most, either way Malley always made out. From time to time this tactic of letting his presence be felt sent a priceless message to his youngin's, that he had their backs and to Larry Gunther and Bobby Cool that he could be hands on at the drop of a dime. This way Larry or Bobby would be aware that repercussions would take place if they allowed their cravings to get high, dictate to cross him in any way. Because all in all, they were crack addicts and their loyalty was to whomever was going to give them their next fix. Risking his money going into the hands of another hustler was one of his pet-peeves. Having his coke in both houses and on the corners was an excellent way to corner the market and a good job of that he was doing. There were plenty of ways to instill fear and Malley vowed to keep taking pages out of Rod's book.

No type of blow back from the cops of any of Malleys' shootings found their way back to him. All he needed to worry about was any attempt of retaliation from either of his foes. A long line of hustlers came from 58th & Filbert and throughout the years the torch was passed from generation to generation. But with every operation in the drug trade, comes the end of a run and then it's on to the next up and coming player. Fifty-eighth Street was wide open and Malley became aware of a few new hustlers who had a knack to get money from that area. Without hesitation and squandering the opportunity to have a piece of 58th Street, he had them moving his product out there as well. The only problem with this corner was that, it stayed hot from the cops or would be robbers attempting to reek havoc. At times Malley would stand out there with them to show his heart and commitment. Putting his product out there was his first step to expanding. Things rolled smoothly for the first month and a half up there. Everything just seemed too quiet and when things were too quiet in the hood, it was probably too good to be true without an act of drama taking place. This sort of sign was never to be ignored. Before any storm, the clouds are present and you could literally smell the tension in the air. Sixty-Second Street raked in it's usual, but 58th Street was like the Dow Jones — ups and downs.

Malley had got a page that 62nd and 58th Street had gotten robbed. He headed over his Aunt Rita's to get with Kaeem.

"What's up J'? Where Ka' at?" he asked, upon entering as J' sat on the couch playing Mike Tyson's Punch Out.

"He upstairs. You alright?" he asked as he saw a disturbed glare in his cousin's eyes.

"Ay, Ka'... ay, Ka'?" he called, nudging him to wake up.

"Yo... What, what's up?" questioned Kaeem half asleep.

"Yo, the duce and the '8' got jammed," he explained angrily.

"What?!" Kaeem asked, surprised as he sat up.

"They took some nice change like, like $8,000 altogether," said Malley, stammering.

"Yeah... Why you have the change layin' around like that?" he asked.

"Naw, L.A. hit me, but I had to take Simone to her mom's job. The other dick heads on the '8' had been supposed to got with me when they ran out," spoke Malley.

"Who you think, Tae and 'em did that?" asked Kaeem, knowing that Tae was going to do everything in his power to bring Malley out into his grasp. The streets was killing Tae's reputation that Malley had shot at him continuously without any repercussions happening to him. He wanted Malley bad. He knew that in order to keep his respect in tact, he was going to have to shoot him. Robbing and shooting his workers wasn't going to save his rep.

"I don't know for sure, but I know it's them niggaz. That's what they do. Plus dude want some get back, bad," Malley stated confident.

"It's a lot of back and forth shit goin' on Mal," Kaeem stated.

"Yeah, it was the bol Tae and 'em," Lil J' said, entering the room, butting into their conversation.

"What? You trippin' what you talkin' about?" questioned Malley, playing dumb.

"Man . . . Oh, I'm a dick head now. Mal, you my cousin and the streets is talkin'. Who don't know Rod passed Market Street off to you," J' said, insulted.

"Naw, it ain't that," spoke Malley, just making up a quick response. Kaeem just sat there without saying a word. He wasn't going to begin to refute with Malley, even though he just tried to pull one over on J'.

"Look, all I'm sayin' is watch ya back out there," Lil J' stressed. Being Malley and Kaeem were closer, he knew that his brother was helping him. But he wasn't going to try and deter Kaeem's loyalty for him because when it was all said and done, they were still family. Lil J' copped a squat and they continued to talk.

"I appreciate that J'. I know one thing Ka', it's on sight with dude and 'em," stated Malley.

"Calm down and think. Don't ever move off of emotions," replied Kaeem.

"Yeah, you right," Malley said, trying to regain his composure.

"You goin' get at 'em, keep ya cool," spoke Lil J' chiming in.

"Damn, I need R' out here. My B.M.'s is gettin' on my nerves. I'm shootin' out every five minutes. Man this shit is crazy," Malley said, now sounding like he wasn't certain he made the right decision to stay in the game.

"Yeah, you might should chill for a minute," Kaeem said.

"I can't, then I'm open season. Muh'fuckas gonna think I'm a pussy and you know the rest. I ain't complainin'. It's just shit comin' at rapid pace. Man, I gotta get some sleep. If S' or Turquoise call and it ain't dealin' with their pregnancy, I'm not here. I gotta get some rest," he repeated, sighing and scratching his head at the same time. Everything as a whole was taking a toll on him. He needed some time to get away mentally.

"Alright," Kaeem said.

He caught up on some sleep, giving his mind and body a reprieve from the ripping and running. His eyes had bags underneath them and they were identically bloodshot like a true Jamaican who didn't do nothing but eat, sleep and smoke weed.

CHAPTER 42

As the summer begin to come to an end, Malley was unsuccessful in touching Tae, let alone finding him. Word on the streets was that Tae had got locked back up for a robbery/shooting and took a deal for 5 to 10 to avoid the 15 to 30 years he was facing. When Malley found that out, he dismissed his losses and kept moving forward. He wanted to keep his promise to Rod by staying in school, so he made it his business to get ready. The semester was beginning Monday and they each had picked their schools. Malley chose Overbrook. Kaeem enrolled in West Philly High and Lil J' elected Bartram. All three of these schools were fashion shows and attracted crowds from the fast lane. West and Bartram had the girls, but Brook was in a class of it's own. The only other school that could give Brook a run for it's money, was Girls High and Central. When it came to the females from Uptown, they stood on their own platform.

Kaeem looked out of the window at the sound of a familiar horn being blown. Malley sat outside in a white Buick Skylark waiting to drop him and J' off at school. Most of the students were catching Septa or letting their parents drop them off. This was a no-no and Malley was going to make sure him and his cousins went to school right on the first day. Only a few other young bols was going to drive in their own car and Malley, Kaeem and Lil J' was going to be amongst those being mentioned. Kaeem and J' made their way out of the house. Lil J' already had a blunt rolled for them, that he brought from 6018. It was 7:40 a.m. and school didn't start until 8:45 a.m., so Malley drove around Gross Street and parked so they could smoke their blunt before they went to school. Each of them were sharp. Lil J' had on all Tommy Hilfiger. Kaeem was in all Polo and Malley put on his Gap sweat suit, which they all had hoe catchers on their feet to match their lay.

"Yo this shit some kill," spoke Lil J' after he stopped coughing.

"Man . . . give me some of that shit," said Kaeem, taking a long deep pull. He turned the tip of the blunt fiery orange. The car quickly began to fill up with smoke as he exhaled. They would always keep the windows up to keep the contact in. It was a myth that you could get higher this way. Malley took his pulls after Kaeem passed him the blunt.

"Yeah, they stay with that gank," spoke Malley, trying to keep the smoke in as long as he was able to. His eyes began to tear up and burn from the smoke. Each of their eyes were chinked and red. The high had sat in. They looked at each other as if they were in another world. The blunt had burned down to the size of a roach. They rolled the windows down, letting out clouds of smoke, while Lil J' tried to take another puff of the blunt only to burn his lips before flicking it out the window.

"Yo, I'm roasted," Kaeem said, licking his lips.

"Yeah . . ." Lil J' said, cosigning the high.

"Yo, we out," stated Malley, starting up the car. It just turned 8:00 a.m. He wanted to drop J' off first because Bartram was over Southwest and he was the farthest away. In fact, it was easier for him to drop Kaeem off on his way to Brook. By the time they got there, 67th & Elmwood was crowded. The girls watched Lil J' get out, analyzing the whole car.

"Yo, we be to get you later, just hit us when you ready," stated Malley.

"Alright," Lil J' responded, heading towards the building.

Next stop was West. By the time he turned on 48th Street it was like a semi-concert out there. The girls were everywhere. Malley dropped Kaeem off right in front of the school so all eyes would be on him. He gave Malley a handshake before he pulled off. Kaeem knew to beep him when he was ready also.

This was the moment Malley anticipated his moment. All four corners was packed and the Suga Bowl had a line coming out of it going towards the corner. Between Ace's Dinner and the Suga Bowl is where everybody would go to eat breakfast or lunch. Malley drove up Oxford Street and parked on Turner. The bell had rung and school had officially started. Everything he had heard about Brook was now presenting itself right before his eyes. He made his way to his advisory class to pick up his roster. It seemed like from every class he went to, or either hallways he walked down, nothing but eye candy after eye candy was around. It was hard for him to choose from which girl he wanted to crack on first, if he optioned to. At this moment he was just feeling things out. He was aware of them checking him out, whispering as he walked passed. This was a role he was all to familiar with playing. Simone was supposed to start at Central but due to the pregnancy, she had to take home school curriculums so she could graduate on time. Turquoise could of cared less if Simone attended. It would of been cat fight after cat fight. Turquoise was always attracted to the fame and she had already had her mind set on watching out for new potential on the prowl for Malley. She was carrying his baby and was going to let the world know he belonged to her; well at least in her mind. Having Simone and Turquoise going to the same school again, with both of them carrying his babies would probably had ended in a travesty.

The first day of school was always like a meet and greet situation that dragged on. After making his way around, finding out where all of his classes were, Kaeem had beeped him. This seemed to be right on time because he was ready to leave anyway. By the time he pulled up in front of West, Kaeem was having a conversation with a bad chick. Malley smirked at the sight of his cousin marking his territory.

"Look, sexy I gotta go, but hit me when you get a chance," he said to her.

"Come on Ka', we gotta go grab J'," he said, interrupting.

"I don't know who he think he is," she said, feeling annoyed by Malley's interruption.

"Chill . . . cool out shorty, that's my brother. He ain't mean it like that," he stated, getting in the car.

"Ka', shorty trippin'. She need to be glad you gave the time and day." Malley confirmed her insinuation, pulling off.

"Damn you peeled on her, you crazy as shit," said Kaeem, laughing hard.

"She luv you long time," he replied.

"You sure you ain't run over her feet?" he questioned, rhetorical.

"Who knows," Malley answered, shrugging his shoulders.

As they pulled up to Bartram, Lil J' was occupied spitting game to a nice looking hottie. It was in their bloodline to attract nice looking girls and be smooth talkers. Kaeem and Malley admired how J' was laying his thing down.

"Yo, come on playboy we out," said Kaeem as Malley stopped the car.

"Alright, look shorty make sure you beep me," J' told her.

"I won't," she responded, smiling.

"Okay I ain't mad at you," spoke Malley.

"Like you really layin' ya mack down," said Kaeem being sarcastic.

"Don't envy me," J' said, responding to Kaeem's remark.

"What we doin' tonight?" asked Kaeem.

"Let's shoot down South Street. It's supposed to be doin' it," suggested J'.

"Whatever, we can shoot down there," said Malley.

Their names were pretty much buzzing in each of their schools. The notoriety of status was having a snowball effect. Malley, Kaeem and Lil J' always tried to be different then everybody else. If certain crews came to school with three quarter length Pelle's. They would throw on the Italian collared Pelle's with gold-studs, flooding the entire leather. The colors didn't matter because they had all flavors. The competition was on. Players from 58th & Willows, Lansdowne Ave, Wynnefield and from 56th to 59th & Master was turning heads also. Putting 62nd Street on the map was a personal task of his. He wanted it to the point to whenever he showed up to an event, they knew he was the bol from 62nd Street. Malley recognized other players in the game, but as long as the respect was mutual he didn't have a problem with giving them their props. Kaeem and Malley took turns driving whips. The girls gave them their own names. They called them; "Them Bols."

CHAPTER 43

Simone had beeped Malley earlier, requesting some strawberry ice cream and some pickles. Malley didn't understand why she wanted pickles and strawberry ice cream. From the beginning of time women religiously craved for the strangest things to eat during pregnancy. Malley walked in the door to Simone talking on the phone.

Here, Rod's on the phone," Simone stated, giving him the phone.

"What's up ol'head?" he questioned, after handing Simone her ice cream and pickles.

"Ain't nothin' youngin',"Rod replied.

"You hear somethin' yet?" he inquired.

"Naw, I'm still waitin' for a decision. The lawyers said it look good though," said Rod.

"That's good money. I can't wait for you to get back out here," spoke Malley.

"Yeah, I know," replied Rod.

"What's up with ya chicks?" he questioned.

"All man . . . they come and go when they want. You know how that go. I'm on they time," he explained to him.

"You have 60 seconds left," the operator announced.

"Damn, we just started talkin'," said Malley, upset.

"Naw, me and Simone was kickin' it before you came in," responded Rod.

"Oh, cause I was about to say they robbin' us out of time. I'm all good out here. I'm in school you know, doin' what I gotta do," he stated.

"I'm proud of you. Just play it down on that situation," stated rod, insinuating the beef between him and Tae. Rod wasn't aware that Tae was already locked up.

"Yeah, I hear you," Malley replied.

"I don't wanna see you in these nut ass camps," said Rod.

"Got you," said Malley.

"You have 15 seconds left," the operator announced again.

"I luv you youngin'," said Rod.

"I luv you too ol'head. You goin' be back out here," Malley said, trying to cram his last words in. He eventually found himself listening to a muted line.

Every time he heard from Rod it made him grind harder. It's nothing more Malley wanted to see other than to have him home. Rod would always sound in good spirits but Malley knew deep down inside, Rod was stressing hard. Not because he was stripped of his lucrative drug operation, but because he was stripped from the ones who mattered the most—his family. Malley had to stop over his mom's to run a couple errands. He gave Simone a kiss on the cheek then left right out. When Malley walked through the door he instantly knew something was wrong. His mother appeared to be sad about something.

"Hey, mom what's up? Is everythin' alright?" he questioned, not knowing what to expect.

"Baby I think you should have a seat," spoke Ms. Jasmine.

"What's wrong?" Malley asked again, wanting to get to the bottom of things.

"Baby . . . it's Turquoise," she said.

"What, I know she ain't get disrespectful with you?!" he asked immediately.

"No, she slipped on some ice and hurt herself," she stated.

"So is she alright?" he asked.

"She's okay but . . ." Ms. Jasmine said, not finishing her statement.

"But what?" he asked, becoming agitated.

"She said she thought she peed on herself, but when she went to change herself in the bathroom she noticed blood was in her underwear," Ms. Jasmine explained.

"So what she ruptured somethin'?" he continued to question.

"Baby, I'm sorry . . . she miscarried," she said with her voice cracking.

"What?!" he asked in disbelief.

"She lost the baby," Ms. Jasmine said, mustering up the ability to tell him. She hugged Malley with all her might. It had hurt her to her heart, having to deliver this devastating news.

"No . . . no . . . mom . . ." he stated, crying out. She maintained her embrace, displaying her motherly love. This was the time he needed her the most. Losing his son before he was born was a mental blow that was going to be hard to recover from. All the street persona went out the door. He cried in his mothers arms like a newborn baby. This took everything out of him and for the first time since he started getting money, he felt helpless, empty and defeated.

Turquoise still had a place in his heart. He spent some time with her at the hospital until she was able to be released. Simone didn't like the fact of him being around her and she dreaded the fact that he had both of them pregnant. But she felt sorry for her as she never wished death on nobody, not her worst enemy or anybody that her enemy loved. Death was nothing to play with because it's never no coming back from it. Kaeem and Lil J' supported him whole heartedly. Rod felt for him as well. He sent his condolences and tried to keep his mind on his current situation. Between Simone's mood swings, the streets and coping with the lost of his son, the fatigue was setting in and he was on the verge of dropping out. Showing up whenever he wanted became the norm. The school would call Ms. Jasmine complaining about his attendance and grades. Every time he was absent this was the routine, even she was getting tired of the calls. Each call got Malley an earful from his mom. Although he was on his own, living with Simone, she still wanted her son to do well in school.

With Rod having a life sentence, the streets wasn't the only ones counting him out. His connect was also.

The material Malley was getting was stepped on to the tee. His work went from grade A to grade Z. The one thing fiends hated the most was inconsistent product and Malley was always known for having good work. The fiends stayed loyal because he always treated them good. But soon his promise of getting back his old product was becoming a dream, putting a dent in his pockets and Rod's power was withering away. On the prowl for a new connect, Malley played it down and would buy 4½ ounces at a time from Turquoise's cousin, Bolo from down North Philly. This was cramping his style because despite him being Turquoise's cousin, he really didn't trust him.

CHAPTER 44

Kaeem had an away game at Brook. The West Philly Speed Boyz played the Overbrook Panthers. This was the first time in a while Malley had gotten to get some fresh air. He really did need a reprieve to take his mind off everything else, that was going on around him. Eager spectators filled Overbrook's gymnasium. Officer Weetly who walked the school's beat in the mornings, stayed overtime to help with security. West and Brook were always rivals on the basketball courts since the days of Wilt Chamberlain. Malley and Lil J' sat right next to each other. Kaeem was warming up with his team, while Overbrook's cheerleaders were performing their routines. The referee blew the whistle and the players lined up against each other anticipating the jump ball. Kaeem and Lamont Greene was going to be sticking each other. Lamont led his team in scoring at the guard position. Kaeem was not too far behind him in points. He just needed to focused some more on his workout drills and put the weed down.

The referee jumped the ball and the Speed Boyz won the tip. The ball went immediately into Kaeem's hand. He pushed it up the court, guarded by Lamont Greene. His other teammates vied for position to get open. Kaeem jabbed stepped a few times, pumped faked then shot a jump shot right in Lamont's face. The ball went straight in the basket, hitting nothing but net. The crowd roared.

"That's my cousin'. He's a fuckin' problem," Malley said excited tapping J'.

Lamont's teammate gave him the ball. Kaeem tried to stay on him like glue, but Lamont was a little stronger than him. He backed him down, turned around face to face with him and crossed him over with his dribble. The crowd cheered as he finished with a lay up. The excitement erupted from both teams, scoring back to back. After the Speed Boyz went on a 10-0 run, they started to pull away, the score was; 44 to 59 with 38 seconds left. Kaeem kept dribbling the ball in place as everybody made their way to the exit. The Speed Boyz had pulled off an upset. The next rival match was scheduled at West. Malley didn't care that they lost, he was there representing his cousin. Lil J' loved the attention he was getting as being Kaeem's brother. The girls would try to go through him to meet Kaeem. His name was appearing in the Daily News, Inquirer and Tribune. His talent was speaking for itself and he was evolving into a high school basketball star.

Malley stopped over Turquoise house. He was still uneasy about loosing his son, so he gave her more attention then he used to. Plus her house was one of his stash spots. He wouldn't keep anything major over there, maybe a few ounces or two. He knocked on the door, anticipating an answer.

"Who is it?" asked Shanda as she opened the door.

"Malley, is Turquoise here?" he questioned.

"Yeah, come in," Shanda said. Shanda and Sonya always stayed over Turquoise's. Her house was their hangout. Malley went straight upstairs. Turquoise was sitting on the bed doing her hair. He was there for one thing and one thing only.

"Yo, grab that bag for me?" he asked. Turquoise went in her closet and gave Malley a City Blue bag contained with coke.

"You comin' back tonight?" she questioned.

"I might," he responded, looking in the bag.

"You ain't gotta look in the bag. I ain't take nothin'," she said, feeling offended.

"Chill," he said.

"Ain't no chill," she replied.

"I mite be back through . . . that is if you don't have reservations with none of ya players," Malley squeezed in, ridiculing her, breaking for the door. She quickly reached for her shoe chucking it at him, trying to hit him in the back of the head.

"I hate you?" she yelled out as he was able to escape the impact of her shoe.

Malley got with L.A and gave him two ounces. One was to go in Larry Gunther's and the other was for Bobby Cool's. Malley was going to put an ounce out on 62nd Street and one on Filbert Street. The streets were dead due to the bad weather from the snow but one thing for sure and two for certain, the fiends would come out to score some crack; rain, sleet or snow and Malley needed his money to keep flowing. Once he dropped everything off he went in the house to spend some time with Simone. Earlier that week Ms. Maxine held a baby shower at her house for Simone. Malley was elated at the anticipation of having his son and Simone's due date was a week away. Malley laid across the bed eating pizza, watching; House Party. That was one of his favorite movies. He was exhausted from all the running he was doing. All he wanted to do was just watch the movie and go to sleep. "Kid N Play" was just battling Shrane and Sidney in dancing. He couldn't wait for his favorite scene, when "Kid N Play" challenged each other in a rap battle. Of course he always knew how it ended with Kid winning, it was just something that was epic to him.

"Malley? Ay, Malley?" Simone called out.

"What? You know my movie on," he responded with his eyes stuck to the television.

"Ain't no what, Rod on the phone," she replied.

"Oh, alright," he said, jumping right up.

"Here," Simone said handing him the cordless phone.

"Yo," Malley said.

"What's up youngin'?" asked Rod.

"Ain't shit, what's up with you?" he questioned.

"Same ol' shit. Yo, the courts just denied my first appeal," spoke Rod, delivering the bad news.

"What we gotta do?" he asked concerned.

"It's cool. The lawyers came to see me and they're on top of it. The District Court was on some bullshit. We're appealin' to the 3rd Circuit, so we should come off there," explained Rod, restoring back hope.

"These muh'fuckas, man . . ." Malley expressed, not completing his thoughts.

"Be cool youngin'. It's far from over. In fact, it just started. I talked to Ka' and Lil J' earlier. They said grandmom and Aunt Rita is doin' fine. How about auntie?" he asked.

"She cool," he replied.

"That's good money. What's up with Simone? When she due?" he questioned.

"That's funny you asked. She due next week," he informed him.

"Well, my prayers is with y'all. Just make sure you send me some flicks when he's born and good lookin' for the flicks of the family," spoke Rod.

"Yeah, that ain't nothin'. You know I was taught by the best," he said, complementing him. Rod smiled from ear to ear on the other end of the phone. Only if Malley could see him.

"Ay look, I gotta save some time to take care of somethin'," said Rod.

"Alright, when you gonna call back?" questioned Malley.

"Probably some time this week," said Rod.

"Alright, I luv you ol'head," Malley told him sincerely.

"I luv you too," he stated before he hung up.

CHAPTER 45

"Malley?" Simone called for him.

"What's up?" he asked, turning around. Simone stood before him with water flowing down her legs.

"I think my water broke," Simone stated.

"What? Ya water broke. What are you talkin' about?" he asked, totally clueless.

"I think I'm goin' into labor. Call Miss Jazzy and my mom. You gotta get me to the hospital," she demanded.

"Oh shit," Malley said grabbing his head. Simone was the one who needed to be panicking not him. He picked up the phone and called his and her mom. They were going to meet them down at Presbyterian Hospital. Malley gathered himself and aided Simone to the car.

As they were escorted straight into the emergency room, the doctors, Ms. Jasmine, Ms. Maxine and Malley stood around Simone as her screams of labor echoed throughout the delivery room. Her labored breathing took a pace of it's own in between each contraction. Signs of exhaustion were definitely apparent. Simone's hair was wildly scattered with beads of sweat covering her face. Malley held on her hand tightly, while Ms. Maxine and Ms. Jasmine spoke to her, trying to keep her calm. Everything seemed to be moving in slow motion for him. Trying to take it all in was overwhelming within itself; doctors, nurses, surgical knifes, bright lights and of course the sight of witnessing Simone endure the excruciating pain of child birth.

"Mommy, I'm in pain," Simone cried out.

"I'm going to give you an epidural," spoke the doctor. He signaled for the nurse to insert the needle into her back.

"You're doin' fine baby," said Ms. Maxine.

"It's almost over baby," stated Ms. Jasmine. Malley was taken aback at the process of the birth.

"Ahh . . ." Simone cried out, still in pain.

"Breathe and push," the doctor ordered.

"Push baby, push," Ms. Maxine told her, rubbing her head. Simone sat up a bit, giving a good push.

"You're doing fine, keep going," the doctor said.

"Ahh . . ." Simone cried out again with a push. The crown of the baby's head was present. Malley's heart began to beat fast as he watched her vagina stretch with each push.

"You're almost there. I can see the head," the doctor encouraged, hoping to guide Simone through a smooth delivery. She continued to listen to the doctor and take short breaths in between each time she had to push. Her mother kept wiping her forehead, while Malley held her hand.

"Stay strong S'," Malley said, just trying to show some support. She looked over at him with a pleased state, then returned back to her agony.

"Push . . . push," said the doctor.

"I am!" she stated out of frustration.

"Here he comes," the doctor announced. He pulled the baby out without any problem. The sound of crying reassured Simone that her son was born. Malley, Ms. Jasmine and Ms. Maxine were beyond excited. The lead nurse wrapped him in a small blanket, wiping the afterbirth off of him. She handed him to Simone. Tears streamed down her cheeks. Ms. Maxine and Ms. Jasmine's eyes filled with tears of joy. Malley had joined the party. The nurse gave him the scissors to cut the umbilical cord. He stood in a semi-trance before he cut it. A flow of emotions owned his face. He felt a strong sense of pride in becoming a father. As his son cried, Simone rocked him back and forth, speaking gibberish to him. The doctor and nurses smiled, admiring the happiness displayed on everyone's face.

"Well, congratulations, you have a handsome son," the doctor said, shaking Malley's hand. Malley was in awe, staring at his splitting image. Simone held her son tightly embracing motherhood.

"Thank you," Malley replied.

CHAPTER 46

Malley and Simone arrived home from Presbyterian Hospital the next day. The doctor wanted to run some tests just to make sure Simone's iron intake was normal. Malley exited the car, helping Simone out and into the house. After such an exhausting delivery she had very little energy to do anything. Ms. Simone and Ms. Jasmine had plans on coming over to help out around the house. They both had hidden agendas of trying to be the first grandmother to spoil their grandson the most.

Malley celebrated with Simone, Kaeem and Lil J' for the first few weeks of the birth of his son, but reality was bills had to keep being paid and food had to be placed on the table for him and his family. Malley still balanced going to school. His full attention of the streets and his son played a major role in his grades. Having the other classmates do his homework was wearing thin. If he didn't practically get straight A's within the next quarter, he surely was going to get left down.

The winter of 92' wasn't the only thing that was fierce on the streets of Philly. The unpredictability of the game was also. You used to be able to see problems coming from a mile away. Now with the new players arriving, altering certain rules, the playing field had gotten slimmer and slimmer. Malley really had to be on his p's and q's if he expected a nice run. No matter what, he refused to let anybody run him away from what Rod left him and continued to build. His heart and his pride kept his momentum alive.

Simone had to go out with Ms. Maxine to take care of some business so Malley was stuck with baby sitting. Before he headed over to his mom's, he double checked the diaper bag for wet wipes, baby food and bottles. She had turned him into a Mr. Mom. He loved having his little man with him. Moreover, Ms. Jasmine was filled with glee each time she was able to babysit her grandson.

"Ay mom, where you at?" asked Malley, making sure his son was secured in the carrier on the table.

"Hey baby, I see you brought my handsome grandson with you," she said, making her way over to little Malley.

"Oh, I don't get no luv no more," said Malley.

"Nope, it's all about my grand baby right now," Ms. Jasmine said, taking her grandson out of the carrier. She held him suspended in air, teasing him with light kisses.

"Mom, everythin's in the bag. He has three bottles and it's like four pampers in there. If you need anythin' just beep me," Malley explained on his way out the door.

"Listen to you, you forgot I was in labor for sixteen hours with you, huh?" she questioned, reminding him.

"Alright mom. Well, me and Simone is goin' to let you and Ms. Maxine take turns watchin' Malley," he said.

"Is that so? Well, I'm glad because she ain't the only one spoilin' my grand baby," Ms. Jasmine said, showing a bit of selfishness.

"Don't worry, you're gonna have him for your vacation. Do you need some money?" he questioned.

"No, you just better be careful out there," she stated, as she kept playing with her grandson.

"Alright, Simone goin' come get him later," Malley said, leaving out.

Malley had got a troubling call from one of his young bols from over Southwest he was giving work to. Kaeem hopped in the car then took the ride with him. He had the young bols hustling for him on Angore-Terrace behind Baltimore Ave. When he pulled up, his young bol was waiting on the porch. Malley and Kaeem got out with their hoodies on. Malley kept his hand in his pocket, wrapped around his gun.

"Yo, what's up?" he questioned immediately.

"Man . . . them niggaz from 57th Street came around sayin' we better shut down shop, so you know we stayed out here. Then they came through cuttin'," his young bol said.

"57th Street? 57th and what?" he asked.

"Warrington," he replied.

"Yeah, did y'all cut back?" questioned Malley.

"You know I played my part," said Lil B.

"Alright, we around there. You sure it was them, right?" he asked.

"I'm tellin' you Mal," his other youngin' replied.

"Alright, we stayin' open, but shut it down for a couple hours. I'ma get with you later," said Malley. Kaeem stood there with no rap. Li1 B hopped in the car with them and they drove off. They headed straight to 57th Street. His new found enemies occupied the corner as Li1 B pointed them out. Li1 B got out the car with Malley. They both were brandishing weapons. Kaeem stayed in the driver side with the car running. Malley was infuriated about them bols shooting at his young bols and trying to shut him down. What he was about to do was against what he believed in, but he had to set an example quick. He wasted no time raising his gun, unloading on everybody who stood on the corner. Lil B. fired right along with him. His foes were running for dear life. A few shots were returned in order to gain cover.

"Come on!" Kaeem said pulling up beside them after they finished shooting. Malley had just broken the cardinal rule of shooting your target. At this point he didn't care. Kaeem turned down Thomas Ave, then took 58th Street all the way back to the Northside. They dropped Lil B off, ditched the car, then went to lay low over Turquoise's.

CHAPTER 47

Turquoise's girlfriend, Teri was spending the night. Teri was a hot looking chick that Kaeem always kept tabs on. She was tight work and he wanted to explore all that she had to offer. They both had on tight jeans with their lips glossed up. Both of their camel toes were protruding. Teri was petite but well filled out.

Turquoise, ya ass gettin' fat," Malley said, wanting to play.

"Boy, stop playin' all the time," she responded, trying to downplay the attention he was showing her.

"Teri you lookin' good ya damn self," said Kaeem, hoping to make her feel comfortable.

"Umm-hmm," she replied to his small complement.

"Well, Ka' give me two el's and I'ma see y'all in the mornin'," Malley said, putting his index finger in her belt loop, pulling her into the room.

"You know I've been tryin' to get at you for the longest," Kaeem spoke.

"Yeah right. You don't act like it, Mr. basketball player," she said.

"Naw, it's true. I just be caught up, but I always ask about you. Turquoise don't be tellin' you?" he asked.

"No," she said.

"Oh, she cock blockin', huh?" he questioned, watching her smile.

"I guess, naw that's my girl she mean well," Teri stated.

"You goin' smoke some of this weed with me?" asked Kaeem

"I don't care," responded Teri.

Turquoise let them use her room. Kaeem sparked up his weed and got comfortable. He loved how she wrapped her pretty lips around the blunt. As the blunt got smaller so did her eyes, the high was kicking in and the ambience created it's moment. Kaeem got closer to Teri, kissing her on her neck with slow soft pecks. As his hands found their way over her succulent breast he could feel her nipples becoming engorged. Her breathing started to pickup. She met his kisses back with her lips before sticking her tongue into his mouth. As she swirled her tongue around tasting his warm flesh, she reached in between his legs grabbing his stiff manhood. Kaeem next pulled her shirt and bra off exposing her 34C mellons. He took his tongue licking around the edges of her areola, sending chills up her spine. This was driving her insane as her brown gum drops stood erect in the air.

Feeling the moisture dampen her panties, she needed to be touched and stroked in her crevasse as the fire continued to grow. Kaeem stripped down to his boxers, sliding a condom on. Teri finally peeled out of her jeans, stepping out of her panties one foot at a time. Her body was immaculate. Her love tunnel was glazed with her juices. Kaeem reached over flickering his finger over top of her clit.

"Oh, that feels so good," she cried out as he picked up the pace.

"You like that?" he asked, making all kinds of variations with his fingers invading her entire vulva. He moved his hands in between her outer and inner labia's.

"Kaeem give it to me . . . stick it in," she begged, hot and bothered. He spread her legs, pinned her knees to her chest and inserted, stroking back and forth. Her tight hole soon became a lubricated entrance.

"Damn, this shit good," he said, continuing his movements.

Malley and Turquoise laid across the bed smoking a blunt. She was in her tight booty shorts. Malley kept smacking her on her fat derriere. In turn she would kick at him playfully. Rather they knew it or not they were indulging in foreplay.

"Ow, stop that hurt," she said laughing.

"Keep your crusty feet off of me," he said, wedging in between her legs. Every time they would share a brief French kiss, she would bite the bottom of his lip as he pulled away.

"You gonna give me my baby," she said, with her legs spread and seriousness within her eyes. Malley did think that he owed her another shot at having his baby because of her miscarriage.

"I feel you babe. Look, let me go get another el from Ka' so we can work on that all night," he stated.

"Alright, hurry up," said Turquoise, putting the pillow between her legs as he walked out.

When he approached Turquoise's room he could hear some muffled rambling. He tapped on the door and to no avail no one answered. As he turned the doorknob, opening it he saw Kaeem and Teri butt naked having the time of their lives. She was moaning out of total bliss. Kaeem had Teri bent over on the bed in doggie style, sexing her out of her mind. You could see his bare ass moving back and forth and her huge titties wobbling all over the place, while he would thrust in and out.

"Oh, fuck this pussy, it's yours," she cried out.

"Who's is it?" he asked, wrapping her hair around the palm of his hand, yanking it and thrusting away.

"Daddy, it's yours. Oh, God you can fuck," she whined.

"I'ma cum in this tight pussy," he told her.

"Go 'head, what you waitin' on?" she questioned, not caring if Kaeem took the condom off or left it on. He was hitting different parts of her walls, causing her body to quiver. Malley was surprised at the way he saw his cousin sexing Teri. Kaeem was slaying her. He gave him inspiration to blow Turquoise's mind. He closed the door quietly and left them to their escapade.

Kaeem and Malley woke up early to go get some breakfast. They were tired of Ace's Diner so they went down 40th & Lancaster to Texas Wieners. The normal sized crowd was waiting in line to order their food.

"Ay yo, I was comin' to grab another blunt from you last night and I opened the door and ya lil ass was givin' Teri the bizness," Malley said, giving him his props.

"Yeah . . . yo, she a freak. I ain't gonna lie. She got some good pussy and her dick suck is crazy. She had my toes curlin' up and all," Kaeem replied.

"Damn, she mean like that, huh?" he questioned.

"Man, we smashed all night . . . I'm feelin' shorty. I need some more of that," Kaeem stated sternly.

"Yeah, I crushed Turquoise last night. She cryin' 'bout another baby," said Malley.

"So you nutted in her didn't you?" Kaeem asked. Malley just looked at him and smiled, knowing he was dead wrong and should be only focusing on Simone and raising little Malley.

CHAPTER 48

"Will you like anything else?" the store employee asked.

"Naw, that's it," Malley responded as she handed him their food.

"Yo, don't turn around . . . but bol and 'em just walked in," said Kaeem trying to keep their identity low.

"Who?" questioned Malley, trying to see their reflection off of the soda machine.

"From 57th Street," said Kaeem. Malley reached for his gun only to remember that he left it in the car. He had to devise a quick plan to allude the ambush. He didn't expect in a thousand years that they would be all the way down there.

"Alright, look we shootin' right to the wheel and we out," said Malley before turning around.

Three of his foes stood by the exit as they had already noticed Malley. Him and Kaeem was going to stick to the plan. As soon as he walked passed them, shots rang out; POP . . . POP . . . POP . . . was all Malley heard before he felt his leg wobble and burn. His platters went everywhere as he continued to run for cover. His foes from 57th Street saw that they hit

Malley and took off. When the shots stopped, Kaeem helped pull Malley into the car, driving off.

"Ah shit! Them pussies shot me!" said Malley, holding his right leg. With fearlessness he looked down at his pierced calf. The bullet went straight through, leaving a tiny gash, exposing his pink and white flesh. The blood trickled a little, dripping down his leg.

"You alright?" Kaeem asked, hoping he wasn't injured too bad. Malley was biting his bottom lip. The pain appeared to be excruciating.

"Ah, shit! This shit burnin'!" Malley said, speaking through his clenched jaw.

"You know I gotta leave you at the hospital," said Kaeem, weaving in and out of traffic.

"Naw, we can't hit the hospital. The law will be all over us. We juvie's, they gotta call my mom," said Malley, making sense out of the situation.

"Yeah, you right, what we gonna do then?" he questioned, as Malley had his seat pushed back, grimacing from pain.

"Hit Turquoise spot," he stated. He understood that going to the hospital or informing his mom and Simone was out of the question. He would of never heard the last of it.

"Alright," Kaeem responded.

Kaeem pulled in front of Turquoise's like a madman. This was a good spot because her mom was never home. He helped Malley limp up the steps. He banged on the door like the police; BOOM ... BOOM ... BOOM ... BOOM ... BOOM ...

244

BOOM ... BOOM ... BOOM! Turquoise swung the door open.

"Boy, is y'all craz ... oh, my God what happened to him?" she questioned, noticing his bloodstained sock.

"Chill, just let me in," Malley said. She quickly followed his demand as he hobbled inside, closing the door behind them.

"Turquoise, we need you to patch him up," spoke Kaeem, sitting him down on the couch.

"What happened?" she asked hysterical.

"I got shot," Malley replied.

"You got shot?! Boy, I ain't no doctor. I don't know how to take a bullet out. You gotta go to the hospital," said Turquoise taken aback.

"Listen, it went straight through. You got some peroxide upstairs?" questioned Malley.

"Yeah, it should be some in the medicine cabinet. It's some iodine in there too," she replied.

"You got some towels and gauze?" Kaeem asked.

"Yeah, everythin's in the bathroom," she said. Kaeem went upstairs to gather all that was needed. Turquoise propped Malley's leg up on the stool, examining his gunshot wound.

"Look all you gotta do is just clean it out for me," said Malley.

"Malley you gotta slow down. Them streets ain't worth gettin' shot over," Turquoise said, displaying her concern.

"I'm good," he responded.

"Here," Kaeem said, returning with the peroxide, iodine and gauze.

Turquoise put on some plastic gloves and poured some iodine on the gauze. She touched his wound, causing him to flinch.

"Sss . . ." he hissed at the burning sensation.

"Don't move, it's gonna burn. I gotta get the germs out," Turquoise stated, wincing at the smell of burnt flesh. She patted his wound gentle each time she cleaned it. Before wrapping it up she dabbed some peroxide on the bandage.

"Good lookin', I need some Ibuprofen and Ka', spark some weed up," said Malley just wanting to relax.

For the first time, Turquoise ultimately had felt appreciated by Malley. Catering and nursing him back to health was a deed she knew that found it's way into his heart. Simone was still leading as she had birthed his son. The only other way to make things even was to have his child and she was going to do everything within her power to make that happen.

Malley hobbled around hiding his gunshot wound as an accident injury. Being as though; it was just a flesh wound, he was able to get away with it. With the profits accumulated after his loses, Malley was able to put $17,000 to the side. Money was to be put up for a rainy day, but in Malley's case, it was storming. He accommodated Turquoise with a small shopping spree for her nursing duties. She was there for him when he needed her the most. She racked up on a bunch of DKNY, Express and a few pair of Keds. Malley even gave her $500 to do whatever she wanted with it. On top of it all, he was still sleeping with her. Turquoise would go to the end of the earth if she had to, just to be able to say that she had Malley's baby. He tried to keep his head in the right place, focusing on his son and Simone. Him and Turquoise's chemistry was too strong for him to tear away from. For some reason she was his Kryptonite and she knew that she was his weakness. Malley refused to allow his leg shot stop him from moving and shaking in the streets.

CHAPTER 49

He laid in the bed next to Simone as she slept peacefully. So much was running through his mind; as his conscious was eating away at him about, not ending the relationship between him and Turquoise. Putting things to an end was the logical thing to do, but he didn't have the willpower to do so. Staring at the ceiling as he drifted away, the sound of his son crying, snapped him out of his dreamy state. He quickly got out of bed to the aid of his son.

"What's the matter, lil man?" Malley questioned, lifting him out of the crib very gently.

"Waan . . . waan . . . waan!" he cried.

"Shh . . . you're gonna wake ya mommy up," said Malley, bouncing with him on his chest. His son continued to cry.

"Waan . . . waan . . . waan!" he cried out again.

"What . . . you, pee-pee or poo-poo?" he questioned, laying his son down, checking his pamper. Come to find out he did neither. His son's crying had awakened Simone. She remained in bed monitoring Malley with her eyes squinted.

"Waan . . . waan . . . waan!" his son whimpered in gibberish.

"Oh . . . ya bottle. You hungry, aren't you lil man,"
said Malley finally figuring it out. He went in the
kitchen turned on the stove, grabbed his milk out of the
refrigerator and warmed up his bottle. He persevered
throughout his cries until he fed him his warm milk.
Little Malley fell right asleep after drinking half his
bottle. Malley lowered him back into the crib then
climbed back in bed. Simone turned over with a smile
on her face, witnessing Malley being a father to his son.
Her heart fluttered with joy as the love of her life and
baby father enforced his role as a family man.

Simone had breakfast ready for Malley when he
woke up in the morning. He didn't have time to eat the
whole plate. He had to check on Bobby Cool and Larry
Gunther's to put some more work in their spots. L.A
was beeping him since 4:00 a.m after they ran out. He
grabbed a piece of toast, kissed Simone and his little
man, then headed for the door.

"Babe I see you later. You too lil man," Malley said
putting up his hands in a boxer stance. He drove
around 62nd Street, dropping an ounce a piece on
Larry and Bobby. That was going to suffice until he was
able to re-up later on.

After he secured the houses, Malley met up with
Kaeem. Before they were going to go to school they
parked and lit up a dime. Kaeem was his right hand and
it was nothing like being in the company of one another.

"Ka' you heard anythin'?" Malley asked, after
taking a puff.

"Naw, I slid through their strip, but they wasn't out
there," said Kaeem, taking his pull.

"We goin' strike . . . I'ma let it die down a lil," Malley replied.

"Yeah, that shit ain't over. They up on us," said Kaeem.

"Yeah . . . nut ass leg shot they gave out. We back over there though, believe that," said Malley inhaling the blunt.

"No doubt," replied Kaeem, double clutching the blunt, then exhaling.

"Yo, it's almost 10:00 a.m.," spoke Malley.

"Yeah, we gotta be out, especially if I wanna get in. Yo, you got ya burner on you right?" questioned Kaeem.

"No doubt . . . yo, I'ma get with you later," said Malley.

"Alright," replied Kaeem, giving him a handshake as he got out of his car, getting into his. They beeped the horn at each other as they both drove away.

By the time Malley had made it up the hill, third period was just beginning to start. That was good for him so it was easy access for him to sneak in the side door as classes changed. As usual Overbrook stayed in sync with it's traditional fashion show trend. The chicks and dudes were draped in the latest. A lot of attention was on Malley as his inconsistent attendance created an Omni-presence, so whenever he did show up, the girls that heard about him were all eyes and ears.

After leaving from a crap game out of the third floor bathroom, a voice he weren't familiar with called out his name. He whipped around only to see a gorgeous young lady.

"What's up sexy, what's ya name?" he questioned smoothly.

"Sania," she answered in a low sweet voice.

"Where you from?" he asked.

"South Philly," Sania replied.

"What you doin' goin' to Brook? Ain't you supposed to be goin' to Bok or Southern?" he questioned.

"Yeah, but I'm usin' my aunt's address," she replied.

"Where at downtown you from?" Malley inquired.

"7th & Mifflin," Sania stated.

"Okay, you down there with Dorian and 'em," he said.

"Yeah they my rodee's," she said.

"Well, won't you write ya number down and I'ma call later," he said.

"Alright," replied Sania, pulling out an ink pen. She wrote it down and gave it to him.

Seventh period came to an end and the students were starting to disperse. Once Malley got to the front door he saw the slush filled and iced streets. A fair amount of onlookers were in the mist of it all. Some were in front of the Suga Bowl, bundled up sipping on hot cocoa, while others stationed themselves across the street at the bus stop, awaiting the G bus to make it's way over the Wynnfield bridge. Old man winter had arrived, but this Friday was like any other, it didn't deter the crowd from the anticipation of the let out. As different crews were broken off into sections, Malley pulled down his skully, rubbed his hands together, blew into them, then placed them in the pockets of his Woolridge as he crossed the street. While he was walking towards his car, which was parked on Turner Street. He noticed some individuals from 60th & Girard were in a pack. His thoughts were so far away from them as possible, being as though Tae was locked up.

"Yo... ya name Malley?" asked Gary with a disgruntled state, who also went by the name of G'.

"Why what's up?" Malley asked, without a worry in the world with his gun concealed on his waist.

"Nigga, you 'bout to find out," G' said, enraged, whipping out his chrome 9mm.

A student in the crowd yelled; "He gotta gun!" Everyone started screaming and running for shelter. Malley darted towards the dumpster. G' wasted no time squeezing his trigger; BLOC...BLOC... BLOC... BLOC... was the sound of the shots he fired. TING... TING... TING... TING... was the sound of the bullets hitting the dumpster. Malley peeped around the dumpster, scrambling to get his gun out so he could return fire; BLOC... BLOC... two more shots rang out before Malley was able to unload his 40 caliber; BLAW... BLAW... BLAW... BLAW... BLAW... BLAW... BLAW! The screams gotten louder as everyone continued to trample over each other to escape the hail of bullets. The Suga Bowl windows were shattered and glass littered the pavement. The sound of gunfire had ceased. What Malley didn't know, was that G' was Tae's cousin and the night that he shot at Tae, he actually hit him in the arm. Being Tae got locked up and couldn't never catch up to Malley, he wanted his cousin to avenge his lost by touching him on sight.

When the smoke cleared, Malley was able to see that G' was laying on the ground wedged in between the drive alley. Blood was rushing out of his neck and chest. After his adrenaline lowered, Malley felt an excruciating pain in his midsection. He stuck his hand in his coat only to drawback, to see his fingers lathered with blood. After realizing he was shot, it drove him straight into shock, stumbling to the ground with his chest burning. Now unable to move and gasping for air, he felt his life slipping away as his heartbeat grew louder as he fought to keep his eyes open; BUMP . . . BUMP . . . BUMP . . . BUMP . . . BUMP . . . BUMP . . .! It sounded in slow motion. With blood gushing out he was loosing consciousness. He could vaguely hear the sirens wailing from the ambulances in distance, along with someone saying; "Stay awake baby, they're almost here!" As he drifted off into another world, memories of his mom, Simone and Turquoise's voice, telling him to slow down kept replaying. The birth of his son and spending time with him taunted his mind.

His body began to get cold as his eyes finally shut, laying there motionless.

Police cruisers were pulling up from all directions. Majority of the cars were from the 19th district. The officers barricaded the crime scene holding the spectators at bay, while the EMT's from the ambulances rushed to G' and Malley. The female EMT checked Malley's pulse. His blood pressure was faint. The male EMT rolled him over on the stretcher and cut his clothes off. He was checking his body for entry wounds, noticing no point of exit. It was a great possibility that he may have been bleeding internally. The female EMT placed a respirator over his face and started an IV as Malley remained immobile. She kept pressure on his wound to try to slow down the outer bleeding. After she was finished. The Male EMT helped her lift him into the ambulance. He rushed around the front, driving off with the sirens blaring and lights flashing, while she stayed in the back with Malley. He was hauled off with his body confined to a stretcher and eyes shut.

COMING ATTRACTIONS

CAUGHT IN THE LIFE!

BY

TEZ

VOLUME 2

PART 4

FLIP SIDE TO THE GOOD SIDE!

CHAPTER 1

With Malley still in a coma state the EMT's whisked him into the emergency room. They're met by a team of nurses and doctors.

"What's his injury?" asked the doctor.

"You have a black male teenager. Gunshot wound to the torso, no sign of exit wound and his pulse is faint," replied the female EMT.

"An IV was started," said the male EMT.

"Where did this take place?" asked the doctor.

"Overbrook High. It appeared to be a shootout. Another teen was also shot," the female EMT responded.

"Okay, thanks. Get him to the 8th floor to begin surgery," the doctor demanded.

Malley was taken to the surgery room. Where he remained unconscious. He was stripped then placed on the operating table. The nurses immediately hooked him up to a heart monitor. His vitals hadn't changed. They removed the respirator and inserted a tube down his throat to help him breathe. The bright lights beamed down over top of him as the team of nurses hovered his body. The lead surgeon was handed a scalpel, cutting a small incision into his midsection. A clamp was stationed to hold his torso open in order for him to retrieve the bullet. The deeper he dug, the faster the blood gushed, causing his body to twitch rapidly. The heart monitor beeped displaying a flat line as his heart stopped.

"Get the defibrillator," the surgeon demanded the nurse. The nurse instantly charged it then placed it on Malley's chest. His body contorted to the first jolt. Without any sign of life. He repeated his action.

"His vitals aren't changing," spoke the nurse, holding the defibrillators.

"Again!" said the surgeon. Malley's body jolted again as the nurse shocked him.

"Nothing," said the nurse, as he rubbed each defibrillator together once more.

"Come on kid . . . God damnit! Don't you die on me! Don't you die on me!" the surgeon spoke enraged, pumping on Malley's chest with both palms. The heart monitor continued to sound — BEEEEEEEEEP . . .

Ms. Jasmine was home washing dishes in the kitchen when the phone rang. When she answered the phone everything went silent. The phone and plate dropped out of her hand in slow motion, hitting the floor. As the plate shattered, she fell to her knees with her hands shaking uncontrollably.

"Not my son. Please God, don't take my son, not now! Not Noooooow!" she yelled out weeping.

DISCUSSION QUESTIONS
QUESTION & ANSWER READER'S
GROUP QUESTIONAIRE

These questions are intended to allow each reader the opportunity to become involved with the storyline and characters.

1. Who is your favorite character and why?
2. Did Malley grow up too fast because of the game?
3. Is Malley wrong for dragging his cousins into situations they shouldn't been in?
4. Do you think Rod's money will get him out of a life sentence?
5. Is Malley wrong for wanting to get Turquoise pregnant again?
6. Do you think Kaeem will keep up with his basketball career if Malley keeps dragging him into the game?
7. Who is more fit for Malley, Turquoise or Simone?
8. Was Malley selfish for not getting out of the game after the birth of his son?
9. Do you think Malley will die?
10. Should Malley get out of the game if he lives?

Post your answers on Facebook & Twitter @ Tez's pages and GoodReads.com

ORDER FORM

Longevity Publishing
P.O. Box 346
Upper Darby, PA 19082
longevityentertain@gmail.com

Name _____

Doc #, if applicable _____

City/State _____

Zip: _____

CAUGHT IN THE LIFE!
By
TEZ
Volume 1
$15.00
Shipping/handling (via media mail)
$3.95
Total: _____

FORMS OF ACCEPTED PAYMENT:
Institutional checks and money orders only

Allow 2-4 weeks for delivery after payment is received.
Order online @ amazon.com, createspace.com,
barnes&nobel.com and smashwords.com
E-books are available on Kindle, Nook, Ipad &
Ibookstore

ABOUT THE AUTHOR

TEZ is a novelist, screenwriter and playwright from West Philadelphia, who has turned his 16-½ years of incarceration into a college and discovered his ability to write. He's created a platform to be able to share his stories with the world. He is the author of the critically acclaimed novel: Caught in the Life! He's penned other works such as Cleopatra, Body Milk, Acronym's of a P.I.M.P. and Ladies in Blue. His screenplays consist of: The Night She Fell in Love (Love/Drama), Dishonorable Gentlemen (Detective/Crime), CooperMart (Comedy), The Jinn (Horror) and 305 (Crime/Drama).

Tez, constantly strives to break barriers and writes about concepts outside of the box. With the completion of five reality show treatments and two TV sitcoms in development, he has no intentions of putting the pen down any time soon, as he continues to study the art of writing and filmmaking. He is also a Board Member and Affiliate of America's Next Big Hit, wwwamericasnextbighit.com. Executive producer and writer with Power Move Multimedia, wwwpowermovemultimedia.com and Nancy Jones Entertainment. Lastly, he is currently working on his latest movie and preparing for his release.

To inquire about a possible interview, collaboration or option of any of his work, please contact him at:

Larry (917) 750-9410
Facebook@tezthewriter
Twitter@tezthewriter
Instagram@tezthewriter
or
Longevity Publishing, L.L.C.
P.O. Box 346
Upper Darby, PA 19082
longevityentertain@gmail.com